BOR

Get **more** out of libraries

Please return or renew this item by the last date shown.

You can renew online at www.hants.gov.uk/library

Or by phoning 0300 555 1387

1116

Hampshire
County Council

ANNE
FRANK

POCKET
GIANTS

ZOË
WAXMAN

Cover image © United Archives GmbH / Alamy Stock Photo

First published 2015

The History Press
The Mill, Brimscombe Port
Stroud, Gloucestershire, GL5 2QG
www.thehistorypress.co.uk

British Library Cataloguing in Publication Data.
A catalogue record for this book is available from the British Library.

ISBN 978 0 7509 5563 8

Typesetting and origination by The History Press
Printed in Malta by Melita Press

Contents

Preface

The Diary of Anne Frank is one of the most famous – and best-selling – books of all time. Yet the girl who wrote it remains an enigma. The real Anne Frank has been hidden again, lost behind the phenomenon of her posthumously published diary.

This concise biography rediscovers Anne. It tells her story from its beginning to its untimely end. It places her life within the wider context of the Holocaust and also explores her afterlife – seeking to explain why, over seventy years after the events it chronicles, Anne Frank's diary still speaks to us today.

Introduction

The Girl Behind the Diary

'I can shake off everything if I write; my sorrows disappear, my courage is reborn.'

Wednesday, 5 April 1944[1]

In honour of the eightieth birthday of Anne Frank, the British Anne Frank Trust – an organisation which attempts to tackle bigotry and prejudice in contemporary Britain – commissioned a pictorial representation of what she might have looked like aged 80. The image shows a rather beautiful woman, displaying the type of gentle wisdom and grace we like to think comes with age and experience. The trouble with the image, which deploys the techniques that are used to artificially age people who have gone missing, is that it bears little relation to what we actually know of the short, sad life of a girl who died of typhus and starvation at just 15 years old in Bergen–Belsen. We cannot know whether or not Anne Frank would have fulfilled her early potential as a talented author or journalist, or how her character might have developed. Her surviving stepsister, Eva Schloss, whom she hardly knew, spoke of her surprise at the image, observing, 'I think she would have been more bitter and disappointed. I didn't see anything of this in the picture.'[2] This photograph and the comment it provoked are indicative of the type of polarised thinking which seems to characterise responses to the life of Anne Frank. Either she is portrayed as heroic and as an example of the triumph of the human spirit, or she is mourned as a tragic victim or icon of suffering.

Anne Frank's fame rests on her diary. She used it – a red and white chequered notebook which she chose herself as a present for her thirteenth birthday – as a confidante. She named it Kitty and it truly did become her best friend. On the first page of the diary, Anne wrote: 'I hope I will be able to confide everything to you, as I have never been able to confide in anyone, and I hope that you will be a great source of comfort and support' (Friday 12 June 1942). She wrote approximately twice a week and dated and signed each entry either 'Anne Frank' or 'Anne'.

The diary, originally written in Dutch and published in 1947 in Holland as *Het Achterhuis: Dagboekbrieven 12 Juni 1942–1 Augustus 1944* (*The Secret Annexe: Diary-Letters 12 June 1942–1 August 1944*[3]), sold only 1,500 copies at the time of publication; but it has since become something of a phenomenon. It has been translated into over sixty languages, from Albanian to Welsh, including Farsi, Arabic, Sinhalese and Esperanto, and has become part of school curricula across the globe. It was added to the UNESCO Memory of the World Register in 2009.[4] Anne Frank's House is the most visited site in the Netherlands and a place where every foreign dignitary is taken. The photographs of her – all taken before she went into hiding

– have become iconic; she has in a sense become the 'face' of the Holocaust.[5] She now even has her own, unofficial, Facebook page.

Frank herself chose the title for the book, which she planned to publish after the war, remarking, 'The title alone would be enough to make people think it was a detective story' (Wednesday 29 March 1944). The original publication title, however, was changed in the 1950 English language edition to *Anne Frank: The Diary of a Young Girl*.[6] It was marketed as the work of an intelligent young girl whose life was tragically cut short. She was just 13 when she began her diary on 14 June 1942, and 15 when she died, becoming one of the at least 1.5 million Jewish children murdered during the Holocaust. Readers of all nationalities and ages felt drawn to Anne and her vivid descriptions of life within the confines of her hiding place. A play, *The Diary of Anne Frank,* written by the Hollywood husband-and-wife team Frances Goodrich and Albert Hackett, premiered on Broadway in 1955 with Marilyn Monroe in the audience, and won the Pulitzer Prize for Drama, the Tony Award for Best Play, and the New York Drama Critics' Circle Award. It was exported all over the world and quickly gave rise to many film versions. In 1996 a feature-length documentary, *Anne Frank: A Life Remembered,* won an Academy Award for best documentary feature. The film contains a very brief sighting of Anne herself leaning out of an apartment window.

Many people had grown up identifying with Anne Frank to such an extent that they felt uncomfortable with the publication of *De Dagboeken van Anne Frank*, an almost unedited version of the diary produced in 1986 by the Netherlands State Institute for War Documentation. A 700-page English translation, *The Diary of Anne Frank: The Critical Edition,* appeared in 1989, reprinting nearly all the different versions of the diary and omitting only the five pages that Anne's father, Otto Frank, deemed unsuitable for publication.[7] It was then translated into German, French and Japanese, and a revised edition was published in Dutch and English in 2003. Willy Lindwer's 1988 international Emmy Award-winning documentary, *The Last Seven Months of Anne Frank*, turned attention to Anne's life *after* her capture. As Anne's testimony stops before her arrest, Lindwer's film is forced to rely on the memories of the Dutch women who knew Anne and her sister Margot in their final months.

Anne Frank's appeal seems in little danger of dissipating. One biographer, Melissa Müller, actually calls herself an 'Anne Frank fan'. As a child she was obsessed by Frank in the same way that other children become fascinated with popular music figures.[8] This is not unproblematic. Anne's diary is a bit like Steven Spielberg's *Schindler's List* (from Thomas Keneally's book *Schindler's Ark*) in that both have become almost totemic of the Holocaust without actually dealing with the reality of life and death in the concentration camps. Both have been used to provide some sort of consolation or antidote to the horrors of the Holocaust. In *Schindler's List* a Nazi collaborator saves Jewish lives, and in many of the various presentations of Frank's diary we are meant to focus on Anne's positivity – her faith in human nature – even in adversity.[9] Although the diary does chronicle the overcrowding, hunger and frustration endured whilst hiding from the Nazis above her father's store in Amsterdam, it stops short of the family's deportation on 4 August 1944. Hence, the diary manages to retain – at least to some extent – the author's zest for life and what Frank herself calls her 'illogical gaiety'.

This book seeks to look again at the life of Anne Frank – a life that we might already think we know. The time is ripe for such an analysis. As the events of that era recede further into the past, we might finally be reaching a point from where we can attempt a more nuanced approach to victimhood during the Holocaust. This means moving away from sentimentality, the sacralising tendency and hushed tones often used to talk about the victims of the Nazi genocide. Without doubt, the life of Anne Frank is a tragedy. She witnessed the murder of thousands of men, women and children; she experienced the murder of her mother; and then watched her sister starve to death before succumbing to the same fate herself. Her death, like every one of the 11 million victims of the Nazi genocide – 6 million of them Jews – represents a life cruelly and brutally extinguished. Yet Frank, who became increasingly aware of the inevitability of her fate, somehow eschewed pathos, and instead produced a most remarkable book. Importantly, she saw her work not just as a private journal, but as an important historical document which would need to be analysed and interpreted in the future.

Whilst the most frequently cited of Frank's statements is 'I still believe, in spite of everything, that people are truly good at heart' (Saturday 15 July 1944), we need to remember that she died a horrible death. We need to remember Anne Frank as a real person: not just a symbol of humanity or the Holocaust but an important figure – and witness – in her own right.

1

The Frank Family

'It's an odd idea for someone like me to keep a diary; not only because I have never done so before, but because it seems to me that neither I – nor for that matter anyone else – will be interested in the unbosomings of a thirteen-year-old school-girl.'

Saturday, 20 June 1942

Anneliese Marie Frank was born in Frankfurt-am-Main on 12 June 1929. She was the second and youngest child of an affluent, cultured, assimilated Jewish family. Her sister, Margot Betti Frank, was born three years earlier on 16 February 1926. Their mother, Edith Frank-Holländer, kept baby books for both children, detailing with great delight their accomplishments and milestones. She dressed the children well, and photographs of their infancy show two very pretty dark-haired little girls with long eyelashes. They looked very much like their mother. Like many mothers, however, by the time her second child arrived, Edith's observations were much less detailed. Anne's father, Otto Heinrich Frank, ran the Bankgeschäft Michael Frank – a bank specialising in stockbroking which he had inherited from his father. Like a great many German Jews, Otto and his two brothers had fought for Germany in the First World War and he thought of himself as German. His mother and sister had worked in hospitals during the war, tending to German soldiers. His family had lived in Frankfurt for centuries and counted many non-Jews among their friends. He was deeply loyal to his country of origin; in many ways his Jewish heritage was of little importance to him. Anne and Margot grew up largely oblivious to the ensuing crisis and enjoyed their childhood years in Frankfurt in their lovely house, which had a big garden with a sandpit, playing with their Catholic and Protestant friends.

Nevertheless, in 1933 when Hitler came to power, Frankfurt became a sea of swastikas. Soon Jewish children were ordered to attend separate schools. The extended Frank family left Germany and its radically escalating anti-Semitism forever. Anne's paternal grandmother, Alice Betty Stern, went to Switzerland, where Anne's aunt and uncle had lived for three years. Otto left for Amsterdam, a city which he knew and where he had friends and business contacts. Once settled, he closed the business in Germany and sent for his daughters and his wife, who arrived at the beginning of 1934. They settled in Merwedeplein, a newly built neighbourhood to the south of Amsterdam housing many other Jewish refugees from Germany. The area still resembled a construction site and the local children were able to play in the huge piles of sand. For Anne, for a short time at least, Merwedeplein was a very happy place. Naturally gregarious, she quickly made friends and spent hours playing outside. The children would go to each other's front doors and ask their friends to play by whistling a tune. Anne, unable to whistle, would sing instead. The girls attended local schools, which helped them to feel part of their new neighbourhood. Margot was the more studious sister; Anne, whilst intelligent, could not stop talking to her friends during classes and was often reluctant to apply herself. This led to some jealousy between the sisters. By the summer of 1934, the family felt settled enough to make frequent trips to Zandvoort aan Zee, a popular seaside town near Amsterdam. Anne and Margot put on bathing costumes and played happily on the sandy beach, eating ice creams. At the same time, newspapers were detailing the escalation of the persecution of the Jews on Polish soil.

The Frank family had managed to bring all their furniture from Germany with them, including some sculptures and other valuable items. This was important for it meant that the family would not have to rely on the Dutch government for financial support. But life undoubtedly became much harder – for Edith especially. The new home was far smaller than she was used to and she no longer had maids to help with the running of the household. She missed German food and German clothes. The shops in Amsterdam were different and she yearned for the cafés where she used to meet her friends. Unlike her daughters, who learnt Dutch very quickly and made many friends, she found the language impossible to master. Without doubt she also worried about family and friends left behind in Germany. On 9 November 1938 – Kristallnacht – 236 people were murdered in Germany and

177 synagogues were destroyed, as well as countless homes and businesses. Following the violence, 30,000 Jewish men were arrested and taken to concentration camps. Among them were Edith's brothers, Julius and Walter Holländer. As a war veteran, Julius was immediately released but Walter remained in the Sachsenhausen concentration camp slightly longer. Eventually they both fled to the United States.

Otto was able to open an agency as part of Opekta-Werke which made and distributed pectin, the powdered fruit extract used to make jam.[10] But he clearly realised that his family were not yet out of danger and in 1937 he tried without success to move his business to England. A year later he attempted to emigrate to the United States but again failed. In the same year he opened a new company – Pectacon – selling spices and other similar ingredients, and he started to look for suitable commercial premises. He eventually located a large building at 263 Prinsengracht, the space where his family would hide for over two years.

Hitler invaded the Netherlands on 10 May 1940, a month before Anne's eleventh birthday. Otto made a final desperate attempt to emigrate to America or Cuba. He did not succeed this time either and his family, along with more than 140,000 Jews – many of them also refugees from Nazi Germany – were trapped.

Although Anne had been brought up to be both very aware and proud of her Jewishness, it had been as a cultural rather than religious identity. Her mother was the only member of the family who went to synagogue regularly. Like the majority of German Jews in Frankfurt, the Frank family had been members of the Liberal Jewish synagogue. The experience of persecution may have heightened the family's cultural or political identity as Jews, but they remained ambiguous in their religious observance. While they were in hiding the Dutch celebration of St Nicholas Day was clearly far more cherished than the lighting of Hanukkah candles. Hanukkah is in fact the only Jewish festival Anne mentions in her diary, though they lit the Sabbath candles every Friday night and enjoyed Jewish food as often as they could.

By the end of 1940, all Dutch citizens had to register with the German authorities and the following year they were issued with identity cards. Any person failing to register had all their property confiscated and was imprisoned for five years.[11] The cards of anyone with more than two Jewish grandparents were stamped with a black 'J'. Signs went up around the city: 'No Jews Allowed.' From May 1941, Jews were excluded from professions such as medicine and law, and they were prohibited from running businesses. Otto Frank devised a plan with his Dutch Gentile colleagues – Johannes Kleiman, Victor Kugler, Bep Voskuijl, and Miep and Jan Gies – to make them the directors of a new company, Gies & Co., which Otto continued to run from behind the scenes. This both protected the business and cemented what would become a crucial bond between Otto and his workers.

By the spring and summer of 1941 Jews were not even able to own bicycles or allowed to use the tram; nor could they visit theatres, cinemas, cafés, museums, public libraries or zoos; and they were not allowed to be outside – even in their own gardens – between the hours of eight in the evening and six in the morning. Anne and Margot were no longer able to go swimming or participate in sports. They were even prohibited from using non-Jewish hairdressers. The worst moment for Anne was when she was forced to move from her beloved Montessori school and her wide circle of friends to a new Jewish school with only Jewish pupils and Jewish teachers; she wept as she said goodbye to her friends and teachers.[12] However, she soon made more friends. In particular she met Jacqueline van Maarsen, from whom she quickly became inseparable; the two girls spent hours together at Anne's apartment. They organised film showings; made tickets and invited all their friends to watch films on the Franks' projector.[13] They also liked frequenting the few ice-cream parlours which still admitted Jews.

Events hundreds of miles away, however, were placing Anne, her friends and her family in more and more danger. In occupied Poland, in Chełmno, in what was to become the first death camp, Jews were murdered in gas vans in December 1941. On 20 January 1942, fifteen senior Nazi officials gathered together in a villa in Wannsee, the once-cosmopolitan suburb of Berlin, to lay out plans for the 'Final Solution to the Jewish question'. Over cognac and cigars the men calmly discussed the subtle distinctions between half-Jews, Jews married to 'Aryans', and war-decorated Jews. Adolf Eichmann, who carefully took the minutes of the meeting, noted plans for the 'evacuation' of Jews to the East.[14] Although it is likely that the decision to murder over 9 million Jews of Europe had already been made, the extermination of Jews from Britain, Ireland, Sweden and the other countries the Germans were yet to occupy presented obvious bureaucratic and logistical problems. Plans were drawn up to transport the Jews to the death camps in Poland via *Sonderzüge* (special trains). All the death camps were conveniently situated along major rail routes.

From May 1942 all Jews in Holland over the age of 6 were forced to wear a yellow Star of David with the word JOOD ('Jew') written in the middle. The star had to be clearly visible and attached to outer clothing over the left breast. Anyone not wearing a star faced imprisonment and a substantial fine. The Jewish star served to make Jews easily identifiable and isolated them from their non-Jewish neighbours. Some non-Jews – at least until they were threatened with deportation – also wore stars as a measure of solidarity. Soon the Jewish neighbourhood where the Frank family lived ceased to be a place of refuge;

instead, members of the Dutch Nazi Party (NSB) prowled the streets destroying Jewish property and attacking Jews at random.

Despite this, Otto and Edith were determined to mark the milestone of Anne's thirteenth birthday on Friday 12 June 1942. It was to be the last birthday she spent before entering the Secret Annexe. In honour of his daughter's new maturity, Otto took her to Blankevoorts, a large bookshop near their home, to choose her present. As we now know, that present was her precious diary. Edith also made Anne cookies to share with her friends at school, and the Sunday following her birthday there was a party with a strawberry pie and the room was decorated with flowers. Her friend Jacqueline remembers Anne's happiness that day: 'With sparkling eyes she had watched her friends enter and opened her presents expectantly. She had enjoyed being the centre of attention.'[15]

Just a week after the party, on Saturday 20 June 1942, Anne wrote: 'You couldn't do this and you couldn't do that, but life went on.' After the war Otto wrote:

When I think back to the time when a lot of laws were introduced in Holland, which made our lives a lot harder, I have to say that my wife and I did everything we could to stop the children noticing the trouble we would go to, to make sure this was still a trouble-free time for them.[16]

By then, news of the atrocities being committed against the Jews was reaching the free world. On 25 June 1942, the *Daily Telegraph* ran a story headed 'Germans Murder 700,000 Jews in Poland'. It detailed the mobile gas chambers and stated that 'on average 1,000 Jews were gassed daily'. Despite the continued reporting of the ongoing atrocities in newspapers such as the *Telegraph*, the *Manchester Guardian* and the *Jewish Chronicle,* Allied intervention was not forthcoming. On Monday 29 June 1942 newspapers throughout the Netherlands announced that all Jews were to be deported to labour camps in Germany. Then, on Sunday 5 July 1942, thousands of German Jewish men and women aged between 16 and 40 received letters via a special mail delivery calling on them to report for the *'Werkverruiming'* ('workforce project') in the 'East', along with a list of clothing that needed to be packed into a rucksack. Among those summoned was Anne's sister, 16-year-old Margot, who would have to leave without her parents and sister and report to the train station at midnight. Margot became quietly fearful and withdrawn. Anne was terrified, but nonetheless was able to retain a child's certainty that her parents could somehow resolve the situation:

> Margot is sixteen – apparently they want to send girls her age away on their own. But thank goodness she won't be going; Mother had said so herself, which

must be what Father had meant when he talked to me about our going into hiding. Hiding … where would we hide? In the city? In the country? In a house? In a shack? When, where, how …? These were questions I wasn't allowed to ask, but they still kept running through my mind. (Wednesday 8 July 1942)

Otto Frank was already in the process of preparing a hiding place for the family. He had put off telling his children both because they might accidentally reveal something to a friend and also because he wanted them to enjoy what little normal childhood they had for as long as they could. He had planned to move them in July, but the summons for Margot meant that the family went into hiding immediately. Although he could not be sure of the terrible fate that awaited those who boarded the trains, Otto was able to listen to the British radio as well as read the newspapers, so he was at least aware that atrocities were taking place on Polish soil. He understood that it was better to try to remain in the Netherlands than be sent to an unknown fate.

People sought a variety of ways out. To obtain a *Sperre* – exemption – many tried to stress that they were essential to the German war effort. Others entered into mixed marriages with Gentiles, although the exemption they were initially afforded proved to be short-lived. Any Jews without connections, or sufficient resources to go into hiding, were forced to comply with the summons. Realising the futility of arguing with the Nazis, the Jewish Council in Amsterdam urged people to report to the station on time. The Hollandsche Schouwburg, a theatre in Amsterdam, came to serve as the antechamber to the concentration camps. Those who decided not to appear were quickly and brutally rounded up by Dutch and German policemen and taken to the Gestapo headquarters. Neighbourhoods were sealed and door-to-door searches were conducted through the night. Otto himself escaped several times by staying the night with friends. Jewish hospitals and orphanages were also the subject of brutal searches.

Otto's decision to keep his family intact was unusual; it was rare for families to go into hiding together. More usually families split up, married couples separated and children went to stay, individually, with Dutch families where they posed as Gentile children or hid within the house. Many of these Dutch Gentiles risked their own and their families' lives without any thought of reward. Others clearly exploited those they claimed to help: financially, physically and sexually.

Children were also placed in orphanages, boarding schools and convents. Some were just a few hours old when their parents gave them to strangers in the vain hope that they might be spared. They could not know when – if ever – they would be reunited. Children who looked 'Jewish' were more likely to be hidden from the public gaze. Others had to dye their dark hair blond and pretend to be Christian. Jewish boys were especially vulnerable on account of their circumcisions. Adults who went into hiding mostly did so by assuming a different, Gentile, identity using cards forged by the Dutch Resistance.

The majority of Jews were, however, captured.

In her book, *Beyond Anne Frank*, Diane Wolf interviews a child survivor who was forced to hide in cellars, attics and even under sinks. The little boy was unable to crawl, walk, or even talk.[17] An entire family staying together was far too dangerous: if one person was betrayed, everyone else was doomed, and more people required greater space and more food. Safe hiding places were difficult to find in the tightly populated towns of the Netherlands, and food was in short supply as it was rationed through a coupon system. The Dutch Resistance Museum in Amsterdam estimates that there were around 300,000 people in hiding in 1944 – more than in any other Western European country. While Jews made up the largest group, students, former soldiers and young men trying to escape forced labour in Germany were also forced into hiding.

The Franks undoubtedly had very strong connections with Dutch Gentile families – as well as having money to offer them – and it is likely that Margot and Anne could have found surrogate families.[18] Anne, in particular, might have found people willing to hide her because, as a young child, she did not need identity papers. Despite this, the

Frank family was committed to staying together – and their wealth enabled them to think that this was possible.[19] Otto Frank was able to rely on his personal finances to support his family in hiding for a long period. Before going into hiding he stockpiled tins of food, soap, rice, jam, flour, tea, coffee and other household essentials. In addition he moved furniture, carpets and valuables to the hiding place. This was despite the decree of 15 September 1941 forbidding Jews from removing furniture from their homes without permission.

Otto knew that with the help of his Gentile friends he would be able to purchase food, clothing, medicine and other necessities for some time to come. As the months in hiding dragged on, the inhabitants of the Secret Annexe at times had to contend with eating nothing but potatoes, spinach or sauerkraut for every meal for weeks on end, but there was little fear of them starving. Unlike most other Jewish families in occupied Europe, the Frank family also had access to a relatively safe place to stay – not in the home of non-Jews, but in Otto Frank's own workplace. It was far from luxurious, but did benefit from a functioning kitchen, a working toilet and separate sleeping quarters. Anne was able to glue postcards of her favourite film stars on to her bedroom walls, as well as pictures of the Dutch royal family and art reproductions.

Miep Gies, Otto's secretary, who, along with her husband Jan, actively participated in the Dutch Resistance, arranged ration cards for people in hiding. They also hid in their own home a young Jewish man who was previously unknown to them. It was with Anne and her family, however, that Miep and Jan formed a particularly close bond. Miep would regularly bring the family not just food, but books and occasional luxuries, including Anne's weekly copy of the Dutch magazine *Cinema & Theater*. After the war Miep was able to recall her emotions on the day of Margot's summons:

> I could feel the urgency, an undercurrent of near panic. But I could see that much needed to be organized and prepared. It was all too terrible. Mrs Frank handed us piles of what felt like children's clothes and shoes, I was in such a state myself that I didn't look. I just took and took as much as I could, hiding the bunches of things the best way I could, under my coat, in my pockets, under Jan's coat, in his pockets.[20]

Miep's dedication to the family was such that even birthdays would continue to be celebrated with cakes, special food, flowers and presents. For New Year's Eve 1943, the helpers threw a surprise party and Miep brought a cake with 'Peace 1944' written on it. They were helped by Johannes Kleiman, Victor Kugler and Bep Voskuijl. Bep was a 25-year-old painfully shy typist who, along with

Miep, worked full-time in Otto Frank's office. In a rare newspaper article after the war, she described some of her life with the Frank family in hiding:

> I ate dinner with the Franks every night. Anne always sat next to me and almost immediately asked if I would keep an eye open for a sturdy notebook where she could note down her daily experiences. It was a shame but in all of Amsterdam I couldn't find such a thing and I therefore gave Anne some blank loose-leaf pages. The child was delighted with this. Once I stayed and slept in the Secret Annexe. Honestly speaking, I was terribly frightened. When I heard a tree creaking or when a car drove along the canal, I became frightened. I was thankful when the morning came and I could once again just return to my work. I can still see Anne crouching here under my desk trying to get a glimpse of the outside world, the street, the canal. Naturally we had to be careful because nobody was supposed to know that there were other people in this building besides the bunch of us in the office.[21]

2

In Hiding

'Although I tell you a lot, still, even so, you only know very little of our lives.'

Saturday, 20 June 1942

Early on 6 July 1942 the Frank family left the home they had lived in for more than eight years and went into hiding in a set of abandoned rooms, ranging over four floors, at 263 Prinsengracht: a long, narrow mercantile house built by the Prinsengracht Canal in 1635. Crucially, it had, like many such buildings, an annexe at the rear. It was in a part of the city that had many warehouses and small businesses and quite unlike the residential area they had been living in. Anne provided a particularly vivid description of that rainy July morning:

> The four of us were wrapped in so many layers of clothes it looked as if we were going off to spend the night in a refrigerator, and all that just so we could take more clothes with us. No Jew in our situation would dare leave the house with a suitcase full of clothes. I was wearing two vests, three pairs of pants, a dress, and over that a skirt, a jacket, a raincoat, two pairs of stockings, heavy shoes, a cap, a scarf and lots more. I was suffocating even before we left the house, but no one bothered to ask me how I felt. (Wednesday 8 July 1942)

Anne also packed a satchel with her diary, her all-important hair curlers, comb, handkerchiefs, school books and letters: 'Preoccupied with the thought of going into hiding, I stuck the craziest things in the satchel, but I'm not sorry. Memories mean more to me than dresses' (Wednesday 8 July 1942). She was particularly sorry that they had to leave behind their cat, Moortje: 'No one knows how often I think of her; whenever I do, my eyes fill with tears' (Sunday 12 July 1942).

The Franks left their home in a state of disarray in an attempt to indicate a forced departure. (It was also rumoured that the family had fled to Switzerland.) As Jews were forbidden from using public transport, Anne and her parents walked the 2.5 miles to their hiding place in the pouring rain in the early morning gloom. Miep and Margot had cycled there even earlier that morning. When they arrived, they found their hiding place filled with their furniture and boxes of food and other supplies. Margot and her mother, soaked to the skin, were too exhausted to do anything but lie down on their unmade beds, but Anne and her father quickly set to work making their new living quarters habitable: 'All day long we unpacked boxes, filled cupboards, hammered nails and tidied up the mess, until we fell exhausted into our clean beds at night' (Friday 10 July 1942). They had no way of knowing that they would remain inside those walls for the next two years.

The Frank family was soon joined by the van Pels family (code-named the van Daans in the diary). Hermann, a colleague of Anne's father – a big outgoing man with a good sense of humour and a quick temper – came with his wife, Auguste or 'Gusti', a house-proud, carefully groomed woman and dedicated, if flirtatious, wife and mother. She was to find life in hiding particularly difficult. It was hard for her to share the running of the domestic life of the attic with Edith Frank and she missed the entertainment and pretty clothes of her former life. Their 15-year-old son Peter, a dark-haired, good-looking boy with bright blue eyes, brought with him his cat, Mouschi. Anne describes their arrival: 'Peter van Daan arrived at nine-thirty in the morning (while we were still at breakfast). Peter's going on sixteen, a shy, awkward boy whose company won't amount to much' (Friday 14 August 1942). Anne was probably a little bit jealous of Peter as he was the only member of the group to have his own room. As if to remind himself of more carefree times he kept his bicycle hung up on his bedroom wall. Later the room would provide a space for Anne and Peter to talk in private and develop their relationship.

The two families later invited Fritz Pfeffer (code-named Albert Dussel), Miep's dentist, who was separated from his Christian wife, Charlotte Kaletta, to join them in late 1942. Anne, who was to share a room with Pfeffer, and inevitably became infuriated by his constant presence, provided the following rather unkind portrait of him:

Trousers that come up to his chest, a red jacket, black patent-leather slippers and horn-rimmed glasses – that's how he looks when he's at work at the little table, always studying and never progressing. This is interrupted only by his afternoon nap, food and – his favourite spot – the lavatory. Three, four or five times a day there's bound to be someone waiting outside the door, hopping impatiently from one foot to another, trying to hold it in and barely managing. Does Dussel care? Not a whit. (Monday 9 August 1943)

Pfeffer was in many ways an easy target for Anne's irritation. He was the only member of the group to have no family with him. He was separated not only from Kaletta, but also from Werner, his son from a previous marriage, who was living in England with his uncle. On top of that, the 53-year-old man had to share a small room with a hyper-critical teenage girl. The pair frequently squabbled over who would get to use the small desk in the room. Margot, who had been sharing a bedroom with Anne, had moved into her parents' room, sleeping on a camp bed which needed to be set up every night. Presumably Anne had at least initially been keen to spend time with someone new – someone who brought with him tales of the outside world.

Both Pfeffer and the van Pels family were German Jews who had become friends with the Frank family, frequently joining them for coffee and cakes on Saturday afternoons. These were not casual gatherings, but specific attempts to bring German Jews together with the Dutch people who might be able to help them. They had also spent a final Seder night together – the ritual feast marking the start of the Jewish holiday of Passover – in April 1942 before going into hiding. Whilst they had been on friendly terms, they could not have imagined what it would be like to have to spend two years solely in each other's company. Not only that, but hidden in a cramped set of rooms next to the office and storeroom where Otto Frank had worked. Crucially, the rooms were hidden from the street. As a further precaution, a month after they went into hiding, Otto asked Johan Voskuijl, manager of the warehouse and Bep's father, to build a swinging bookcase in front of the plain grey door and the steep wooden staircase that led to the entrance of the Secret Annexe. They lived there in fear of air raids, of the Nazis, of intruders and thieves, and of the ordinary Dutch citizens who might at any moment decide to betray them.

Anne's early diary entries record what was significant to her at the time and stress the importance of her life before she went into hiding. She writes about her classmates, her school activities and her recent birthday celebrations. Little mention is made of the German occupation and the events that drove her family into the attic. She wrote:

It's really not that bad here, since we can do our own cooking and can listen to the wireless in Daddy's office. Mr Kleiman and Miep, and Bep Voskuijl too, have helped us so much. We've already preserved loads of rhubarb, strawberries and cherries, so for the time being I doubt we'll be bored. We also have a supply of reading material, and we're going to buy lots of games. Of course, we can't ever look out of the window or go outside. And we have to be quiet so the people downstairs can't hear us … Yesterday we had our hands full. We had to pit two crates of cherries for Mr Kugler to preserve. We're going to use the empty crates to make bookshelves. (Saturday 11 July 1942)

The occupants of the Secret Annexe lived in a perpetual state of fear that they would be discovered. The curtains had to remain closed at all times and the windows were covered by blue paint. They all had to be out of bed and washed before the warehouse workers arrived at half past eight to avoid unnecessary movement – Margot and Mr van Pels both longed for the luxury of a 'hot bath, filled to the brim, which they can lie in for more than half an hour' (Friday 23 July 1943). The rooms were narrow, which made them feel even smaller than they really were. Eight people and only one toilet and sink added to the stress. It was difficult to make people hurry as they all craved the solitude of the toilet as the one place they could go to be alone. Laundry and cleaning could only be done on Saturday afternoons and Sundays when the warehouse was closed. During the week, when people were in the store below, they had to move quietly and speak only in whispers. Disagreements were whispered and any stirrings of emotion hastily silenced. Anne and the others could not use the toilet or turn on a tap. They had to wear slippers and avoid making any noise on the creaking floors. Even dropping something could risk discovery. Pepper floating up from the shop's grinding machines caused them to sneeze, but this too had to be done as quietly as possible. Once it was dark – and in winter this was as early as four o'clock – they could not even read. As the neighbours of the Secret Annexe were also a source of possible discovery, they still had to remain cautious at night. Each time a new worker started there was heightened apprehension. During the group's occupancy the warehouse was burgled several times, each time bringing a further risk of discovery and increased vulnerability. On 1 March 1944 Anne wrote:

The only explanation is that the burglar must have had a duplicate key, since there were no signs of a forced entry. He must have sneaked in early in the evening, shut the door behind him, hidden himself when he heard Mr van Daan, fled with the loot after

Mr van Daan went upstairs and, in his hurry, not bothered to shut the door.

Who could have our key? Why didn't the burglar go to the warehouse? Was it one of our own warehouse employees, and will he turn us in, now that he's heard Mr van Daan and maybe even seen him?

It's really scary, since we don't know whether the burglar will take it into his head to try and get in again. Or was he so startled when he heard someone else in the building that he'll stay away?

Many of the adults smoked, and the air in the attic became increasingly foetid. As the war progressed and cigarettes were harder to come by, tempers became frayed. The rooms of the attic were piled with belongings. For Anne, her place of refuge soon felt like a prison: 'Not being able to go outside upsets me more than I can say, and I'm terrified our hiding place will be discovered and that we'll be shot' (28 September 1942). As they were residing in an old canal building, rats and mice were also plentiful. The claustrophobia was almost unbearable. Anne was unable to see the sky, could not feel rain or sun, walk on grass, or even walk for any length of time. Instead she studied the big chestnut tree outside her attic window.

With the enforced passivity and increasingly poor diet, the health of the inhabitants of the Secret Annexe declined, their physical strength decreased and their immunity lessened. Deprived of natural sunlight, Anne suffered from a deterioration in her eyesight and they all experienced tooth decay. Then in the winter of 1943 she had a particularly bad case of influenza from which she took a while to recover. Even coughing was dangerous: 'With every cough, I had to duck under the blanket – once, twice, three times – and try to keep from coughing anymore' (Wednesday 22 December 1943). Had anyone in hiding become dangerously ill, there would have been little that could be done for them. Anne was fearful:

> The atmosphere is stifling, sluggish, leaden. Outside, you don't hear a single bird, and a deathly, oppressive silence hangs over the house and clings to me as if it were going to drag me into the deepest regions of the underworld. At times like these, Father, Mother and Margot don't matter to me in the least. I wander from room to room, climb up and down the stairs and feel like a songbird whose wings have been ripped off and who keeps hurling itself against the bars of its dark cage. (Friday 29 October 1943)

Otto Frank had been shrewd enough to realise that boredom would be a potential danger. He was himself an intellectually engaged man with interests ranging from photography to German literature. He made sure that life in the attic was subject to a strict schedule. Anne spent a great deal of time studying and reading the books that Miep brought her each week – particularly European history and literature. She had managed to bring 'a large supply of exercise-books, pencils, rubbers and labels from home' (Monday 21 September 1942). Otto also read aloud to the children – the books of Dickens and the plays of Goethe and Schiller. When Anne was on her own, however, she liked to read romantic fiction and mythology. Anne, Margot and Peter also kept up with their studies through correspondence courses. Margot, the most studious of the children, took a Latin course using Bep's name as an alias; her teacher was unaware that she was corresponding with a Jewish girl in hiding for her life. All three children studied French and Edith Frank took an English correspondence course. Fritz Pfeffer studied English, Spanish and Dutch without, as Anne put it, 'noticeable results' (Tuesday 16 May 1944).

Anne hoped against all odds that she would one day be able to return to school and dreamt of going on to spend one year in Paris and another in London, studying the history of art, learning languages, seeing 'beautiful dresses' and 'doing all kind of exciting things'. Whereas Margot wanted one day to become a maternity nurse in Palestine, Anne hoped to become 'a journalist, and later on, a famous writer' (Thursday 11 May 1944). In preparation for this role she amassed a book of her favourite literary quotations, including Goethe and Oscar Wilde, and a separate notebook for new, potentially risqué words such as 'brothel' and 'coquette' (Saturday 27 February 1943).

Indeed, as well as her diary, Anne left behind a notebook of short stories labelled 'Verhaaltjes en gesbeurtenissen uit het Achterhuis' ('Tales and Events from the House Behind') which, unlike her diary, have only been translated into a handful of languages. The stories mostly focus on things that happened whilst she was in hiding. One of them, 'The Battle of the Potatoes', describes the feuds that developed over the dwindling food supplies. She also used the notebook to initiate conversations with Peter, for whom she had developed romantic feelings. As Anne went from being a child to a young woman, all within the confines of the Secret Annexe, she ceased to find Peter 'quiet and boring' (Friday 5 February 1943). On 8 November 1942 Peter turned 16. His burgeoning maturity was marked by suitably sophisticated gifts such as a board game, razor and cigarette lighter. Anne observed: 'Not that he smokes so much, not at all; it just looks so distinguished' (Monday 9 November 1942).

Like many young people she also worried about her appearance, studying her face in the mirror and asking her sister for appraisals of her looks. Margot had always been the more classically beautiful child with her tall, slim figure and quiet good looks. She took care with her appearance and even her eye glasses were considered fashionable. Anne, on the other hand, was quirkier, with dimpled cheeks and deep-set grey-green eyes that dominated her small face. She spent time curling her dark hair, manicuring her nails and even bleaching with hydrogen peroxide the dark hairs that grew above her top lip. Not without humour, Anne writes that, after finishing in the bathroom, 'The next person in invariably calls me back to remove the gracefully curved but unsightly hairs that I've left in the sink' (Wednesday 4 August 1943). She also lists the toiletries she dreams one day of buying: 'powder, skin cream, foundation cream, cleansing cream, suntan lotion, cotton wool, first-aid kit, rouge, lipstick, eyebrow pencil, bath salts, bath powder, eau-de-Cologne, soap, powder puff' (Wednesday 7 October 1942). Rationing in Holland meant that even soap was hard to come by.

In due course Anne and Peter played out the dramas of young love, moving from a first kiss to the inevitable cooling of their feelings in their confinement. Describing the momentous occasion of the kiss, Anne wrote:

He held me firmly against him, my left side against his chest; my heart had already begun to beat faster, but there was more to come. He wasn't satisfied until my head lay on his shoulder, with his on top of mine. I sat up again after about five minutes, but before long he took my head in his hands and put it back next to his. Oh, it was so wonderful. I could hardly talk, my pleasure was too intense; he caressed my cheek and my arm, a bit clumsily, and played with my hair. Most of the time our heads were touching. (Sunday 16 April 1944)

The young couple discussed whether they should reveal their relationship to their parents and Anne decided to confide in her father, who in turn spoke to Peter about the importance of keeping their feelings under control. Anne was not looking for her father's permission to continue her romance, but rather desperately needed to discuss her newly emerging sexual feelings. She was unable to speak to her friends and unwilling to speak to her rather overprotective mother. Although she did confide in Margot – the two exchanged letters about Peter – she was clearly aware of how lonely Margot must have felt as her younger sister spent happy hours talking with the only other young person in the Annexe. In one letter, which Anne reproduced in her diary, Margot confessed:

Anne, yesterday when I said I wasn't jealous of you, I wasn't being entirely honest. The situation is this: I'm not jealous of either you or Peter. I'm just sorry I haven't found anyone with whom to share my thoughts and feelings, and I'm not likely to in the near future. But that's why I wish, from the bottom of my heart, that you will both be able to place your trust in each other. You're already missing out on so much here, things other people take for granted. (Monday 20 March 1944)

However, Peter was unable to satisfy Anne's desire for intimacy, for someone who could truly understand her. She explained, 'Peter is kind and good, and yet I can't deny that he's disappointed me in many ways. I especially don't care for his dislike of religion, his talk of food and various things of that nature' (Tuesday 13 June 1944). The shortcomings of the relationship were no doubt heightened by the fact that the entire romance was conducted within the increasingly claustrophobic conditions of the Secret Annexe. Peter and Anne were unable to do the simplest things such as enjoy the sunshine or walk hand in hand through a park.

Peter, a naturally energetic boy, doubtlessly suffered greatly in the Secret Annexe, not least because he must have been particularly affected by the limited meals. Anne observed that 'even after the most substantial meal' he 'could have eaten twice as much' (Monday 9 August 1943). As time went on, meals in the Secret Annexe dwindled. Less fresh food was available in the shops and at far higher prices. Money was needed to supplement ration cards. The van Pels family, in particular, were running out of money fast and trying to sell their possessions. Miep even tried without success to sell Peter's bicycle. Peter was also just a boy who, like Anne, found himself impotent to change his situation. Ultimately it was still to her father that Anne turned for comfort and reassurance. Each night the inhabitants of the Secret Annexe would lie awake listening to the Allied and German planes flying overhead shooting at each other. Anne wrote: 'I still haven't got over my fear of planes and shooting, and I crawl into Father's bed nearly every night for comfort. I know it sounds childish, but wait till it happens to you! The ack-ack guns make so much noise you can't hear your own voice' (Wednesday 10 March 1943).

During this period Miep and Bep were also bringing news of the deaths and deportations of friends and acquaintances. The Jews of Europe were being systematically segregated from the rest of the population and sent to their deaths in 'the East'. In 1943 the death camps of Belzec, Sobibór, and Treblinka were established, killing between 1.5 and 2 million Jews. Each time Miep and Bep came to the attic with food and other necessities, Anne and the other occupants of the Secret Annexe bombarded them with questions, the answers to which could only add to their fears. It was impossible to keep from them what was going on in the outside world. Kleiman remembered: 'When we had our plate of soup upstairs with them at noon, we tried to say nothing about what was happening outside. But it could not be concealed. The air was charged with it. It penetrated through the walls.'[22] Also, the very fact that Miep and Bep were able to bring less and less food and other items into the Secret Annexe spoke of the deteriorating situation in Holland. Whilst the helpers were clearly doing their best in increasingly difficult circumstances, there was tension when the inhabitants of the Secret Annexe felt they were being kept in the dark. Relying on others for their every need created a sense of dependency which was not always easy to accept. It is almost impossible to feel continually grateful.

Anne was sensitive enough to realise this. Whilst she was aware that her very survival was dependent on the helpers, she also nursed an understandable jealousy of their freedom:

Miep and Mr Kugler bear the greatest burden for us, and for all those in hiding – Miep in everything she does and Mr Kugler through his enormous responsibility for the eight of us, which is sometimes so overwhelming that he can hardly speak from the pent-up tension and strain. Mr Kleiman and Bep also take very good care of us, but they're able to put the Annexe out of their minds, even if it's only for a few hours or a few days. (Friday 26 May 1944)

Anne was also quietly envious of Kleiman's daughter, Jopie. Jopie, who could not be allowed to know that the Frank family were not, as she had been told, 'abroad' but in hiding in Amsterdam, was free to fall in love, play sport, see friends – all the things Anne so badly wanted to be doing. She wrote: 'I don't think I'm jealous of Jopie, but I long to have a really good time for once and to laugh so hard it hurts' (Friday 24 December 1943). Anne was intensely aware of how 'fortunate we are' compared 'to other Jewish children' (Friday 24 December 1943), yet it was nevertheless impossible for her to always feel grateful and not be envious of children who had not been born Jewish. It was also hard for her to get used to an existence bereft of the material comforts she had grown up taking for granted. The lack of soap powder meant that bedding could not be laundered and everyone's clothing was becoming increasingly 'old and worn' (Sunday 2 May 1943). Margot, she reports, is forced to wear a bra two sizes too small (Sunday 2 May 1943). Anne's own vests were 'so small they don't even cover my stomach' (Sunday 2 May 1943).

Like most adolescents, Anne felt a certain disdain for her family, perhaps exacerbated by the claustrophobia of her rapidly shrinking world. She wrote in March 1944: 'Every day I'm growing cooler and more contemptuous of Mother, less affectionate to Father, and less willing to share a single thought with Margot' (Thursday 16 March 1944). The next day she continued, 'it's been quite a blow to suddenly realize that very little remains of the close and harmonious family we used to be at home!' (Friday 17 March 1944). At the same time Anne was aware that her outpourings were 'simply expressions of anger that, in normal life, I could have worked off by locking myself in my room and stamping my foot a few times or calling Mother names behind her back' (Sunday 2 January 1944). Indeed, some of her complaints are heartbreakingly mundane: 'Whenever I go upstairs, they ask what I'm going to do, they won't let me salt my food. Mother asks me every evening at eight-fifteen if it isn't time for me to change into my nightie, and they have to approve every book I read' (Friday 17 March 1944).

Anne also complained that Mrs van Pels hoarded the clean linen to prevent those who are not her family from using it. She was probably not completely conscious of the fact that both her mother and Auguste van Pels were becoming increasingly depressed the longer they spent in hiding. Anne herself was taking valerian daily for anxiety and depression. Auguste, who was by nature a lively woman with a good sense of humour, was becoming increasingly withdrawn and obsessed by her dwindling material possessions. Edith Frank not only found Auguste hard to live with, but was growing more fearful of the fate that awaited them outside the attic and was trying – albeit unsuccessfully – to quell her anxieties by increased attention to her daughters.

Anne was finding the behaviour of the adults around her more and more difficult to bear. Fuelling the tension was the inevitable heightened sensitivity to the subtle changes of the others' moods. Anne wrote: 'Father walks around with his lips pressed together, and whenever he hears his name, he looks up in alarm, as if he's afraid he'll be called upon to resolve another delicate problem' (Sunday 17 October 1943). For Anne's mother it was acute awareness of the disapproval of the other adults towards her daughters that caused her particular distress. Like most mothers she could not bear people thinking her children had been badly brought up. Even when they were not quarrelling, the boredom of seeing the same people, day in, day out, was stultifying. Anne wrote:

> Whenever one of the eight of us opens his mouth, the other seven can finish the story for him. We know the punch line of every joke before it gets told, so that whoever's telling it is left to laugh alone. The various milkmen, grocers and butchers of the two former housewives have been praised to the skies or run into the ground so many times that in our imaginations they've grown as old as Methuselah: there's absolutely no chance of anything new or fresh being brought up for discussion in the Annexe. (Friday 28 January 1944)

Desperate to broaden her world, Anne used her father's binoculars to look out at what was going on below. She did not find the sight particularly edifying: 'The people in this neighbourhood aren't particularly attractive to look at. The children especially are so dirty you wouldn't want to touch them with a bargepole. Real slum kids with runny noses. I can hardly understand a word they say' (Sunday 13 December 1942). She was equally engrossed in the daily fights over food. On Thursday 30 December 1943 she wrote:

> Since the last raging quarrels, things have settled down here … Nevertheless, a few dark thunderclouds are heading this way, and all because of … food. Mrs van D. came up with the ridiculous idea of frying fewer potatoes in the morning and saving them for later in the day. Mother and Dussel and the rest of us didn't agree with her, so now we're dividing up the potatoes as well. It seems the fats and oils aren't being doled out fairly, and Mother's going to have to put a stop to it … For the last few months now we've been splitting up the meat (theirs with fat, ours without), the soup (they eat it, we don't), the potatoes (theirs peeled, ours not), the extras and now the fried potatoes too. If only we could split up completely!

Without doubt, Anne saw her writing as a creative and emotional outlet, a very personal project. But when, on 28 March 1944, the inhabitants of the Secret Annexe listened to Gerrit Bolkestein, the Dutch Minister of

Education, Art and Science who was exiled in London, state in a BBC programme broadcast illegally by Radio Oranje (the voice of the Dutch government-in-exile) that after the war he wished to collect eyewitness accounts of the experiences of the Dutch people under the German occupation, she started to see the wider significance of her writing. The day after the broadcast, she wrote: 'Of course, everyone pounced on my diary. Just imagine how interesting it would be if I were to publish a novel about the Secret Annexe' (Wednesday 29 March 1944).

On 20 May 1944 Anne began rewriting and editing her diary on loose sheets of paper given to her by Bep, making improvements, omitting those sections she did not think would be of interest, or which she thought might be potentially embarrassing – such as complaints about her mother and observations regarding her own burgeoning sexuality and her first menstrual periods. She did this at the same time as keeping her original, more private diary. The idea that her experiences would be historically interesting allowed Anne to see herself as more than a suffering child; at the same time she knew all too well that she was just one voice amongst many. She was very much aware of the catastrophe unfolding across Europe and took pains to list the growing number of anti-Jewish laws. She knew that there was a Jewish ghetto near to where her family hid and had witnessed the deportation of the Jews of Amsterdam to the Westerbork transit camp from her attic window:

In the evenings when it's dark, I often see long lines of good, innocent people, accompanied by crying children, walking on and on, ordered about by a handful of men who bully and beat them until they nearly drop. No one is spared. The sick, the elderly, children, babies and pregnant women – all are marched to their death. (Thursday 19 November 1942)

After being violently dragged from their homes and detained in local buildings, the beleaguered Jews were transported to Westerbork and then to the death camps in Poland. Listening along with her family to the nightly radio broadcasts of the Dutch government-in-exile, she became aware of the mass slaughter of Jews taking place on Polish soil. A diary entry on Friday 9 October 1942 stated:

Our many Jewish friends and acquaintances are being taken away in droves. The Gestapo is treating them very roughly and transporting them in cattle-trucks to Westerbork, the big camp in Drenthe to which they're sending all the Jews. Miep told us about someone who'd managed to escape from there. It must be terrible in Westerbork. The people get almost nothing to eat, much less to drink, as water is available only one hour a day, and there's only one lavatory and sink for several thousand people. Men and women sleep in the same room, and women and children often have their heads shaved. Escape is almost impossible; many people look Jewish, and they're branded by their shorn heads.

With a sense of foreboding, Anne described her attempts to sleep: 'Sleep makes the silence and the terrible fear go by more quickly, helps pass the time, since it's impossible to kill it' (Friday 29 October 1943). At the same time fear and the enforced passivity of the attic made sleep harder to come by. Every little sound caused Anne to wake in terror and she then found that the infuriating presence of Pfeffer made it impossible to go back to sleep: 'First, there's the sound of a fish gasping for air, and this is repeated nine or ten times. Then the lips are moistened profusely. This is alternated with little smacking sounds, followed by a long period of tossing and turning and rearranging pillows' (Wednesday 4 August 1943).

When they first went into hiding, the Frank family might have hoped that the war would be relatively short-lived and that they could return to the life they had once led, but they were soon to realise that this was increasingly unlikely:

Countless friends and acquaintances have been taken off to a dreadful fate. Night after night, green and grey military vehicles cruise the streets … It's impossible to escape their clutches unless you go into hiding. They often go around with lists, knocking only on those doors where they know there's a big haul to be made. (Thursday 19 November 1942)

One night, in a dream, Anne sees her childhood friend Hannah Elisabeth Pick-Goslar (Lies Googens in the diary) amongst the damned:

I saw her there, dressed in rags, her face thin and worn. She looked at me with such sadness and reproach in her enormous eyes that I could read the message in them: 'Oh, Anne, why have you deserted me? Help me, help me, rescue me from this hell!' (Saturday 27 November 1943)

By the end of 1943 the vast majority of Jews in the Netherlands had been deported. Only about 5,000 Jews ever returned – approximately 20 per cent – the highest death rate in Western Europe. The sense of terror in the Secret Annexe was mounting. On Wednesday 29 December 1943, Anne wrote: 'Why do I always think and dream the most awful things and want to scream in terror?' The inhabitants of the Secret Annexe clung desperately to some hope of a reprieve from their increasingly inevitable fate. Otto Frank, listening daily to Radio Oranje and the BBC, followed the progress of the

Allied forces. On a small map of Normandy that he had cut out from the daily newspaper *De Telegraaf* (*Telegraph*), he marked their movements with little red pins. On Tuesday 6 June 1944, Anne declared:

> A huge commotion in the Annexe! Is this really the beginning of the long-awaited liberation? The liberation we've all talked so much about, which still seems too good, too much of a fairy tale ever to come true? Will this year, 1944, bring us victory? We don't know yet. But where there's hope, there's life. It fills us with fresh courage and makes us strong again. We'll need to be brave to endure the many fears and hardships and the suffering yet to come.

It was not to be. Two months after the Allied landings in Normandy the police discovered the Secret Annexe. Anne had reached the end of her luck.

3

Capture

'I am afraid of prison cells and concentration camps.'
Sunday, 12 March 1944

On a beautifully sunny day, 4 August 1944, three days after Anne's final diary entry, the Gestapo – headed by Karl Josef Silberbauer – arrested Anne together with the other inhabitants of the Secret Annexe.

Otto had been helping Peter with his schoolwork. Silberbauer spotted an old army footlocker on which Otto's name and rank in the German Army were printed. He expressed his admiration that Herr Frank had fought in the Great War. It made no difference. In another room Margot cried while Anne and her mother stood with their hands up. The Frank family had spent a total of two years and thirty-five days in hiding.

Betrayed by an anonymous source who had reported their existence to the Nazi authorities, the inhabitants of the Secret Annexe were forced into a windowless police truck and taken to the headquarters of the Sicherheitsdienst (SD or Bureau of the German Security Service of the SS), where they were interrogated. Otto Frank insisted that he did not know of any other Jews in hiding. He was believed. Miep Gies followed them and tried unsuccessfully to buy their release. Instead, they spent the next three nights at Huis van Bewaring, a large, brutally ugly prison in Weteringschans, in central Amsterdam. Also arrested were Victor Kugler and Johannes Kleiman, who had been helping them; they were imprisoned in Amsterdam – and survived the war. Miep and Bep were not arrested and continued running the business. It seems that as women they were considered unlikely to have been actively involved.

Kugler remembered the last time he saw those he had tried so desperately to save from such a day: 'At a distance, in the corridor outside Silberbauer's office, we saw the Franks, the van Pelses and Pfeffer. All eight looked serious and troubled, not knowing what the future would bring. We waved to each other and that was goodbye.'[23]

Four days later the eight prisoners were taken to the central train station in Amsterdam and transferred to Westerbork, the transit camp in the province of Drenthe, in the northern part of the Netherlands, guarded by the Dutch regular and military police.[24] Otto Frank recalled:

We rode in a regular passenger train. The fact that the door was bolted did not matter very much to us. We were together again, and had been given a little food for the journey. We knew where we were bound, but in spite of that it was almost as if we were once more going travelling, or having an outing, and we were actually cheerful. Cheerful, at least, when I compare this journey with our next. In our hearts, of course, we were already anticipating the possibility that we might not remain in Westerbork to the end. We knew about deportation to Poland, after all. But then, were not the Russians already deep in Poland? The war was so advanced that we could begin to place a little hope in luck. As we rode toward Westerbork we were hoping our luck would hold. Anne would not move from the window. Outside, it was summer. Meadows, stubble fields, and villages flew by. The telephone wires along the right of way curvetted up and down along the windows. It was like freedom. Can you understand that?[25]

Their arrival in Westerbork ended any hope.

The camp, which was surrounded by a barbed-wire fence and watch towers, was situated in a particularly bleak part of the country. After having to strip naked and have their bodies searched for valuables, the former inhabitants of the Secret Annexe were labelled 'convict Jews' on account of having been in hiding. They were placed in the punishment barracks, where they received even less food than prisoners in the main camp. The men had their hair shaved while the women had theirs cropped; and then all prisoners were given blue overalls with red shoulder patches and wooden clogs in place of their civilian clothes. Then, beginning at 5 a.m. each morning, they were forced to toil for hours cleaning old aeroplane batteries in a dirty workshop where they were exposed to chemicals. Children such as Anne were sent to the cable workshop. Soap was not to be had in the camp. For lunch they were given a small piece of stale bread and thin soup. This was labour with the sole purpose of destroying the strength and morale of the worker. According to those who remember the Frank family at that time, Anne became increasingly fearful and clung to her mother and sister. Although Otto lived in the men's barrack he was frequently able to visit his family. Yet again he tried to reassure his daughters with remembered stories and hopes for a better world.

Perhaps if they had possessed any hope that they would survive the war, the hardships of Westerbork might have proved more bearable. However, the threat of deportation to somewhere worse was omnipresent. In his diary of Bergen–Belsen, Abel Herzberg, a Dutch lawyer and writer who was imprisoned in the camp, wrote:

Westerbork was another word for purgatory. There was nothing to sustain one, materially or spiritually. Each was thrown on his own resources, utterly alone. Desperation, total and absolute, seized everyone. People sought help but seldom found it and, if they did, knew that it could not possibly prevail. Deportation to Poland might at best be postponed – for a week, perhaps, or for a few weeks at most. Husbands were powerless to protect their wives, parents had to watch helplessly while their children were torn away from them forever. The sick, the blind, the hurt, the mentally disturbed, pregnant women, the dying, orphans, new-born babies – none were spared on the Tuesdays when the cattle-trucks were being loaded with human freight for Poland. Tuesdays, week in, week out, for two interminable years.[26]

Between the summer of 1942 and the autumn of 1944 a train 'to the East' departed each Tuesday morning filled with men and women going to an unknown future. People fought desperately to avoid the transport, but to no avail. On 3 September 1944 the former inhabitants of the Secret Annexe were put on the very last train from Westerbork. By that time 100,000 Dutch Jews had already been taken to either the Sobibor or Auschwitz–Birkenau death camps, along with over 200 gypsy peoples – Roma and Sinti. When Canadian troops liberated Westerbork on 12 April 1945 they found just 876 Jews remaining there.

Up to seventy-five people were packed into each cattle truck without access to fresh air, food, water or toilet facilities. The small bucket for water was soon emptied and the larger bucket used for a toilet soon overfilled, leaving a terrible stench in the airless train compartments. Fights broke out as people became increasingly desperate. When they reached their final destination three days later the dead outnumbered the living. Janny Brandes-Brilleslijper, a member of the Dutch Resistance, was in the same car as the Frank family. She remembers:

> The longer the trip lasted, the more belligerent people became … the kindest, gentlest people become aggressive when they've stood for a long time. And you get tired – so terribly tired – that you just want to lean against something, or if possible, even if only for a minute, to sit down on the straw. Then you sit on the straw and they step on you from all sides because you are sitting so low. All those feet and all that noise around you make you aggressive … And then you, too, push and hit.[27]

In his memoir Otto wrote: 'The awful transportation – three days locked in a cattle truck – was the last time I saw my family. Each of us tried to be as courageous as possible and not to let our heads drop.'[28] The fear and discomfort was such that they could not even sleep. Amazingly, five people actually managed to escape from the train. They made a hole in the wooden floor of the boxcar and lowered themselves through the gap. They were injured, but survived.

Otto Frank wrote: 'I can no longer talk about how I felt when my family arrived on the train platform in Auschwitz and we were forcibly separated from each other.'[29] On arrival at Auschwitz, under glaring searchlights, *kapos* (prisoners in charge of work) and SS guards accompanied by fierce dogs shouted at them through loudspeakers to disembark the train. Men and women were separated and roughly shoved into rows of five. Whips were used to instil order. Anne, Margot and their mother were then subjected to the usual selection procedure where those judged unfit to work – the elderly (people over the age of 50), the weak and children under the age of 15 – were never registered, but were immediately sent to their deaths in the gas chambers. Young children who had gone into hiding without their parents met their deaths alone. It is estimated that in this way approximately 865,000 Jews were sent straight to the gas chambers. The majority had no idea of the fate that awaited them until it was too late. More people were murdered at Auschwitz than at any other camp – at least 1.1 million men, women and children perished there, 90 per cent of them Jews. It has been reported by the Dutch Red Cross that of the 1,019 men, women, and children on the Franks' convoy train, only forty-five men and eighty-two women survived.

Anne had just celebrated her fifteenth birthday and was relatively fit and healthy, so she was spared. Along with her mother, sister and Auguste van Pels, she made the walk to the women's camp at Birkenau where around 39,000 prisoners were held. Otto Frank, together with Hermann van Pels and Peter, went to the men's camp. He never saw his wife and daughters again. Hermann – the first of the eight to die – perished in the gas chambers just a couple of weeks later, aged 54. The exact date of his death remains unknown. Peter witnessed his father being led away. When Otto ended up in the sickbay barracks, Peter, who worked in the postal department of Auschwitz, visited him daily, bringing with him the additional food he managed to obtain as part of his privileged employment.

As the Soviet Army approached, the Germans began dismantling the gas chambers and destroying the camp. Peter was put on a death march to the Mauthausen concentration camp. He survived the arduous journey but, according to the Red Cross, died in the camp on 5 May 1945, aged 18, just three days before the camp was liberated by the Soviets.

Fritz Pfeffer was part of a transport of physicians and dentists sent from Auschwitz to the Neuengamme concentration camp near Hamburg. The conditions were terrible and he was made to engage in particularly gruelling physical labour digging the Dove–Elbe canal. He died in the hospital barracks on 20 December 1944 at the age of 55. Whilst nominally delineated as a place for the sick, the hospital barracks at Neuengamme lacked even basic medical care. Instead, prisoners with a variety of different and often contagious diseases were left to die together. Otto somehow managed to survive Auschwitz. When he was liberated he weighed a mere 115 pounds.

Those spared an immediate death in the gas chambers of Birkenau were led into a low, narrow building, made to discard their clothes and hand over any last possessions. They then had their heads, underarms and pubic areas shaved before receiving an ice-cold shower. In a further effort to dehumanise the victims, their names were replaced with anonymous numbers tattooed on their arms. The Dutch women on the transport which included Edith, Margot and Anne were tattooed with numbers from A-25060 to A-25271. Prisoners were then given either blue-and-white striped uniforms or the clothes of previous arrivals deemed not good enough to be distributed to Germans. Alternatively, they were given the uniforms of Russian soldiers who had perished in Auschwitz or, occasionally, clothes of a mockingly unsuitable nature, such as ball gowns or flimsy evening dresses. Edith, Margot and Anne received sack-like tunics with crosses on the back to show that they were new arrivals. They had nothing to wear underneath. All the clothes were filthy and many were bloodstained.

Then, as new prisoners in Auschwitz, the Frank family were placed 'in quarantine', where rations were especially slim and conditions particularly harsh. They were housed in one of the many identical blocks overfilled with sick and hungry women. Prisoners had to fight for a place on the wooden bunks and were frequently forced on to the filthy floors. In Auschwitz everything needed to be fought for – from the bowl that prisoners needed to hang on to if they were to be fed, to the rancid soup placed in it, to their very survival. New arrivals were despised by the veteran prisoners, who were envious of the longer amount of time they had spent in the free world. Unlike many of the prisoners, the Frank family had not come from the ghettos of Eastern Europe and were therefore totally unprepared emotionally, intellectually and physically for the shock of the camps. They had to quickly learn how to negotiate the soup queues in order to obtain 'thicker' soup, and to work out whether it was better to eat their entire bread ration and tiny piece of margarine at once or nibble it throughout the day; they also had to learn how to defend it from stronger prisoners. In addition, they needed to realise that it was essential to try to keep clean: to wash with the morning's ersatz coffee and remove the lice from their clothes. Many prisoners could not adapt to their harsh new surroundings and either gave up the fight for survival and went obediently to the gas chambers or threw themselves on the electric fence that surrounded the camp.

Anne developed scabies – a condition where lice get under the skin leaving excruciatingly itchy red and black sores – and was sent to the *Krätzeblock* (scabies block) where the risk of being transferred to the gas chambers was particularly high. At this time both Edith and Margot could have left Auschwitz to work in a Czechoslovakian munitions factory, but they refused to go without Anne. Unlike many other prisoners they refused to turn their back on their daughter and sister. Indeed, Margot volunteered to join her sister in the *Krätzeblock*, where she inevitably developed the ailment herself. Edith desperately tried to obtain additional food to feed her daughters. Ronnie Goldstein van Cleef, who was also in the *Krätzeblock,* recalled:

> The Frank girls looked terrible, their hands and bodies covered with spots and sores from the scabies. They applied some salve, but there was not much that they could do. They were in a very bad way; pitiful – that's how I thought of them. There wasn't any clothing. They had taken everything from us. We were all lying there, naked, under some kind of blankets. Two of us shared a blanket, lying in a single cot.[30]

Then, in October 1944, as the Soviet Army approached Auschwitz, Anne, Margot and Auguste van Pels were once more put on a train to an unknown destination: this time the concentration camp Bergen–Belsen back in the Frank family's native country of Germany. The journey lasted four days with minimum rations in the freezing cold. Yet again, Anne and Margot had no idea where they were being taken. Auguste was ferried to Buchenwald and then to Theresienstadt. An eyewitness report suggests that she was thrown under the train on that transport, where she died, aged 44. Edith Frank, who had fought tirelessly to protect and feed her daughters, died in the sickbay barracks in Auschwitz–Birkenau on 6 January 1945, also aged 44. Those who knew her in her final days say such was her distress at being separated from her beloved daughters that she had given up the fight for life and was barely lucid.

Bergen–Belsen was originally set up by Heinrich Himmler in 1943 as an internment camp for Jews who were to be held as hostages to be exchanged for German nationals in Britain and America. Only a handful were ever exchanged, however, and by 1945 Jews from all over Eastern Europe were being sent there. Although Bergen–Belsen was a concentration camp and not a death camp (which meant it lacked gas chambers and the means to systematically murder its victims), by the autumn of 1942 conditions in the camp had become so poor and the overcrowding so great that a major typhus epidemic broke out, leading to the deaths of thousands of prisoners.

Anne and Margot were placed in a tent camp where the living conditions were particularly miserable. Even water was a scarce commodity – the SS liked to amuse themselves by turning off the water supply – and prisoners fought each other to drink from any dirty puddles on the ground. Food was practically nonexistent – unless you counted the Red Cross food parcels rotting in the camp storerooms – and there were several reported cases of cannibalism.

On 15 April 1945 when the British Army liberated the camp, they discovered around 10,000 unburied corpses lying on the ground. The task of separating the living from the dead and dying was almost impossible. The 60,000 survivors continued to die from starvation and disease in the months following liberation. The British soldiers, appalled by what they witnessed, quickly handed out their rations to the starving survivors, who gorged themselves on the rich, tinned food. Unfortunately, their weakened stomachs were unable to digest the tins of steak and kidney pudding and suet deserts and many prisoners succumbed to diarrhoea, which in their fragile states proved fatal. According to some estimates, approximately 2,000 prisoners died from being given the wrong food after liberation.[31] The British liberators had to burn down the camp to prevent the spread of further disease. Lieutenant Colonel Gonin of 11 Light Field Ambulance described the appalling sights they encountered:

One saw women drowning in their own vomit because they were too weak to roll over and men eating worms as they clutched half a loaf of bread purely because they had to eat and could now scarcely tell the difference between worms and bread. Piles of corpses, naked and obscene, with a woman too weak to stand propping herself up against them as she cooked the food we gave her over an open fire. Men and women crouching down just anywhere relieving themselves of the dysentery which was scouring their bodies, a woman standing naked washing herself with issue soap in water from a tank in which the remains of a child floated.[32]

The British journalist Richard Dimbleby was among the first to report the atrocities. He described how a desperate woman screamed at the sentry for milk to feed her baby before thrusting it into his arms and running off. 'When he opened the bundle, he found that the baby had been dead for days. This day at Belsen was the most horrible of my life.'[33] Dimbleby found himself too distressed to complete the radio report and his eyewitness testimony was not broadcast until several days later as the staff at the BBC found it almost impossible to believe.[34]

Anne's childhood friend, Hannah Elisabeth Pick-Goslar, said that when she met Anne at the camp: 'It wasn't the same Anne. She was a broken girl.'[35] Rachel van Amerongen-Frankfoorder, who had first met the Frank family in Westerbork, and re-encountered Anne and Margot in Bergen–Belsen where they were in the same barracks, remembered:

The Frank girls were almost unrecognizable since their hair had been cut off … And they were cold, just like the rest of us. It was winter and you didn't have any clothes. So all of the ingredients for illness were present. They were in bad shape. Day by day they got weaker … The Frank girls were so emaciated. They looked terrible. They had little squabbles, caused by their illness, because it was clear that they had typhus. You could tell even if you had never had anything to do with that before.[36]

Typhus is a wasting disease which affects the brain, causing ravings and delirium. It results in an agonising death. Anne and Margot somehow managed to survive just over four months in Bergen–Belsen before succumbing to malnutrition and typhus a few months before the camp was liberated. Anne was just 15 years old and Margot 19.

Janny Brandes-Brilleslijper witnessed the last days of Anne and Margot:

At a certain moment in the final days, Anne stood in front of me, wrapped in a blanket. She didn't have any more tears … And she told me that she had such a horror of lice and fleas in her clothes that she had thrown all of her clothes away. It was the middle of winter and she was wrapped in one blanket. I gathered up everything I could find to give her so that she was dressed again. We didn't have much to eat … but I gave Anne some of our bread ration … Two days later, I went to look for the girls. Both of them were dead! First, Margot had fallen out of bed on to the stone floor. She couldn't get up anymore. Anne died a day later. We had lost all sense of time. It is possible that Anne lived a day longer.[37]

Hannah Goslar stated that Anne told her, crying, 'I don't have any parents anymore'. She added, 'I always think, if Anne had known that her father was still alive, she might have had more strength to survive.'[38] Ultimately, however, the women who knew Anne and her sister at this terrible time can say little more than that she suffered like the rest of them, and died like many thousands before her, a terrible death.

The emaciated, typhus-ridden bodies of Anne and Margot Frank ended up with thousands of other nameless victims in a mass grave – one of a series of mass graves at Bergen–Belsen, each one holding up to 5,000 corpses. The horrific mass of skeletal bodies made indistinguishable by intolerable suffering were once loved and cherished individuals. As it was impossible to bury so many bodies manually, bulldozers were used to shovel them into the graves, often splitting the bodies as they did so. Local people were brought in and forced as punishment to witness the devastation that had been wrought whilst they were engaged in the mundanities of their everyday lives in the charming town of Belsen. They were made to dig more graves, toiling in the merciless sunshine along with the thirty SS women, Hungarian guards and handful of SS men left behind after the more senior guards had fled. Today, each grave is marked by a simple stone façade inscribed with the number of dead bodies the grave contains. There is in fact no way of knowing in which grave their remains lie and it was not until 1990 that a memorial was created specifically for Anne and Margot Frank at the site of the former concentration camp. It has since become a place of pilgrimage. Visitors to the site leave gifts – flowers, stones, cards, soft toys, flags and even jewellery. Each week they are collected and archived in the museum at Bergen–Belsen.[39]

4

The Diary

'I do talk about "after the war", but then it is only a castle in the air, something that will never really happen again. If I think back to our old house, my girlfriends, the fun at school, it is just as if another person lived it all, not me.'

Monday, 8 November 1943

Anne was forced to abandon her precious diary on 4 August 1944 when the Secret Annexe was raided. Miep Gies and fellow staff member Bep Voskuijl hastily managed to rescue it – three notebooks and some loose sheets of paper scattered on the floor along with some schoolbooks and photo albums of the Frank family.[40] Miep hoped against hope that she would one day be able to return Anne's diary to her. Importantly, she did not read it at this time but put it away in an unlocked desk drawer for the rest of the war. Years later she explained: 'Had I read it, I would have had to burn the diary because it would have been too dangerous for people about whom Anne had written.'[41] Indeed, one of the reasons that diaries such as Anne Frank's are so rare is because of the fear that they could be discovered during a raid.[42] Just a week after Miep rescued the diary, the Gestapo ordered the clearance of the Secret Annexe. All the furniture and belongings of the people who had hidden there became 'property of the Reich' and was shipped to Germany.

Otto Frank, the only surviving member of the family, returned to Amsterdam via Odessa and Marseille on

3 June 1945 and was immediately reunited with Miep and Jan Gies, with whom he would live for the next seven years. Although he already knew that his wife was dead, he clung to the hope that, as Bergen–Belsen was not a death camp, his daughters had somehow managed to survive. Miep and Jan shared his conviction that the two girls would one day return.

As survivors of the camp started to filter back to Amsterdam, Otto questioned every former prisoner he came across. He pored over the lists of survivors compiled by the Red Cross (both the Red Cross and the Dutch Department of Social Affairs conducted extensive research into the deaths of Dutch citizens during the war) and placed adverts in newspapers. Two months after his return to Amsterdam, Otto discovered his daughters' fate from Janny Brilleslijper, who had also returned to Amsterdam. On 7 July 1945 he wrote to his mother and brothers with confirmation that Margot and Anne had died in Bergen–Belsen. He alone had survived.

Otto returned to the Secret Annexe and was confronted with emptiness. All the families' possessions had been cleared. He decided the rooms should always remain empty as if to signify the loss of those who had once lived there. It was then that Miep, who had kept Anne's writings in the hope of one day returning them to their author, gave them to her father instead, saying: 'Here is your daughter Anne's legacy to you.'[43] She still had not read them. It was some time before Otto could. He wrote to his mother: 'I don't have photos from the last years of course, but Miep by chance saved an album and Anne's diary. But I didn't have the strength to read it.'[44] Instead he tried to keep his businesses going – as much for his loyal employees as for himself – until, in 1952, at the age of 63, he retired and moved to Switzerland. There he later married Elfriede Geiringer-Markovits, herself a survivor of Auschwitz. He died in 1980 at the age of 91, leaving the original copies of his daughter's diary to the Netherlands State Institute for War Documentation. The diary is now on display in the Secret Annexe.

At first Otto had no intention of publishing Anne's diary but wished only to share those parts he considered important with surviving family and friends. He translated sections of it into German to send to his mother in Basle, Switzerland. When friends and family began suggesting that he consider having the diary published, he started editing it – rather as Anne had done herself – deleting critical comments about his dead wife and the other inhabitants of the Secret Annexe as well as the passages dealing with Anne's growing sexuality. He then typed a more extensive version of the diary, combining Anne's original diary with the version she herself rewrote, and including within it four stories from her notebook. He took the manuscript to the Dutch historian Annie Romein-Verschoor, who shared it with her husband,

Jan Romein, a professor of Dutch history at the University of Amsterdam.

In April 1946, after several Dutch publishers had rejected the manuscript, Jan Romein published an article in the Amsterdam newspaper *Het Parool* praising the diary and its rich account of wartime life. The article, entitled 'A Child's Voice', was printed on the front page of the newspaper. It described Romein's experience of reading the diary for the first time:

> By chance a diary written during the war years has come into my possession. The Netherlands State Institute for War Documentation already holds some two hundred similar diaries, but I should be very much surprised if there were another as lucid, as intelligent, and at the same time as natural. This one made me forget the present and its many calls to duty for a whole evening as I read it from beginning to end.
>
> When I had finished it was nighttime, and I was astonished to find that the lights still worked, that we still had bread and tea, that I could hear no aeroplanes droning overhead and no pounding of army boots in the street – I had been so engrossed in my reading, so carried away back to that unreal world, now almost a year behind us.
>
> It is written by a Jewish girl who was thirteen years old when she went into hiding with her parents and

an older sister and began this diary, and it ends one wretched day more than two years later when the Gestapo discovered the whole family. One month before the Liberation she died in one of the worst German concentration camps, not yet sixteen.

How she died, I do not wish to ask; it was probably described in so many camp reminiscences …

The way she died is in any case not important. What matters far more is that her young life was wilfully cut short by a system whose witless barbarity we swore never to forget or to forgive while it still raged, but which, now that it belongs to the past, we are already busily, if not forgiving, then forgetting, which ultimately comes to the same thing.[45]

The article brought much-needed attention to the diary, and in June 1947 Uitgeverij Contact, a small Amsterdam publisher, published 1,500 copies of *Het Achterhuis*, with a preface by Annie Romein-Verschoor and an extract from Jan Romein's article on the dust jacket. It got rave reviews.

Although Otto was able to arrange for a French edition in the spring of 1950 and a German edition a few months later, initial sales remained low. It was not until the appearance of the English edition a decade later that the book became a bestseller, inspiring adaptations on the stage and screen. Otto encountered many who thought that the diary should never be published – those who argued that it was too personal and that it was wrong to commercialise his daughter's memory – yet he remained convinced that Anne would have wanted her name in print and her diary to be read by as many people as possible. After all, her greatest wish was to be a famous writer. He could never bring himself to watch a theatrical interpretation of the diary, however. As he wrote to the cast of the Goodrich and Hackett production: 'For me, this play is part of my life and the idea that my wife and children and I will be presented on the stage is a painful one to me. Therefore it is impossible for me to come and see it.'[46] Indeed, he became embroiled in an argument (which lasted many years) with the American novelist Meyer Levin over the theatrical adaption of the diary.

As the diary of Anne Frank became increasingly famous it took on a new aura and gained something of the status of a mystery. Not only is there the fact that the diary survived whilst its author did not, there is also the tragic truth that despite all we now know of the life and death of Anne Frank, we cannot know the exact details of her final resting place.

In 1986, after receiving Anne's diary, bequeathed to it by Otto, the Netherlands State Institute for War Documentation produced *De Dagboeken van Anne Frank*, a compilation of Anne's original diary (with just a few omissions), her revised version of the diary and the already published version of it. This critical edition includes the report by the State Forensic Science Laboratory of the Ministry of Justice summarising a series of tests to confirm that the ink, glue, cloth cover and writing implements used in the diary do indeed date from the early 1940s and are the authentic, intellectual property of Anne Frank. Such conclusions contradicted the suggestions of prominent Holocaust deniers such as Robert Faurisson, a French professor of literature. In 1978 he published an article entitled, 'Is the Diary of Anne Frank Genuine?' in the *Journal for Historical Review*. He went on to publish a series of prominent opinion pieces in *Le Monde* questioning both the authenticity of the diary itself and also the claims made by the author within it. He declared Otto Frank to be 'a literary fraud' and concluded that the diary was 'a "cock and bull story", a novel, a lie'.[47] In a second article published in the *Journal for Historical Review* Faurisson made a further series of accusations against Otto, mostly focusing on the alleged financial gains he made from the diary.[48] Faurisson is but one of many to level these charges.

Whilst it is clear that Holocaust deniers have a specific agenda in attempting to cast doubt over the diary of Anne Frank – if her diary can be called into question so can the historical fact of the murder of 6 million Jewish men, women and children – there is still a lot we do not know about the arrest of the inhabitants of the Secret Annexe. In 1948 a police investigation set out to discover who had betrayed them. Miep Gies, Victor Kugler and Johannes Kleiman identified Gezinus Gringhuis and Willem Grootendorst as the Dutchmen working with the German Security Service who had made the arrests. They were sentenced to life imprisonment. In 1963 the famous 'Nazi hunter' Simon Wiesenthal tracked down Karl Silberbauer – who had already served a short prison sentence for his role in the Gestapo – and he was identified as the officer in charge of the arrests. His defence was the well-trodden line of 'just following orders', which extraordinarily was supported by Otto Frank, and he was exonerated. Otto wanted to honour the legacy of his family by promoting the ideals of tolerance and forgiveness. He had always been a deeply ethical man and he did not want his tragic experiences to change this. Otto, who testified at Silberbauer's trial, stated: 'The only thing I ask is not to have to see this man again.'[49]

The following year Wiesenthal set out to discover who had told the Dutch police of the existence of the Secret Annexe in the first place. The Frank family had been careful to inform all their friends and acquaintances that they had successfully escaped to Switzerland, and both the van Pels family and Fritz Pfeffer had done as much as they could to erase any trace of their continued existence in Amsterdam. Whilst both investigations pointed the finger at Willem van Maaren, the warehouse supervisor in charge of Otto's businesses, he categorically denied even knowing about the existence of the eight people in the Secret Annexe and his role in the arrests could never be proved, although it is clear that the inhabitants of the Secret Annexe had frequently discussed their concerns about him. He was also suspected of carrying out a series of petty thefts of food items.

Van Maaren cannot be the only suspect, however. It is quite possible that someone living nearby saw something – a chink of light through a window, for example. The Nazis offered substantial rewards to those who supplied information leading to the arrest of Jews and, as the war progressed and economic conditions worsened, many Dutch citizens became tempted to betray their former friends and neighbours. The *Police Gazette* published the names of 'missing' Jews. Others betrayed the Jews not for money but because they were committed anti-Semites. And others, more banally, did so because they believed in obeying the law. Anonymous letters were written informing the police where people were hiding or who was in the Resistance. But, to this day the identity of the person responsible for the arrest and deportation of the eight people hiding in the Annexe remains elusive.

5

Celebrity

'I want to go on living even after my death.'

Wednesday, 5 April 1944

There are now 'Anne Frank tours' which guide tourists from her childhood home in Frankfurt and the plaque commemorating the house where she was born, on to Amsterdam, and then to the transit camp at Westerbork, before proceeding to Auschwitz and Anne's final resting place at Bergen–Belsen. Anne Frank's hiding place became a public museum on 4 May 1960 after attempts to demolish it to make way for new office developments were thwarted. Even before the official opening of the museum, visitors had flocked to the building, asking if they could look around. (Most visitors are unaware that in 1634 the exiled French philosopher René Descartes had found refuge in that very neighbourhood.) Visiting the house today – a short tram ride from Amsterdam Central Station – it is almost impossible to believe that eight Jewish men and women were in hiding there for fear of their lives. More than a million people make the pilgrimage to the Anne Frank House museum at 263 Prinsengracht each year, including the Canadian singer Justin Bieber, who caused outrage in 2013 by writing in the guestbook that, had Anne Frank lived, 'hopefully she would have been a belieber'.

The actual attic where Anne wrote most of her diary is closed off to visitors and, at Otto Frank's request, the rest of the rooms have remained unfurnished. Visitors are nevertheless encouraged to feel a sense of intimacy with Anne's life in hiding. Squeezing through the false wall built behind the bookcase, one cannot help but feel a sense of trepidation mingled with excitement. Climbing the narrow staircase to the Annexe where she lived, one is transported back to her world. You see the photographs of the film stars – Greta Garbo, Ginger Rogers – that Anne glued on her makeshift bedroom wall, Otto Frank's map of Normandy, and also the pencil marks – now covered with glass – which show how much Anne and her sister Margot grew during their two years in hiding. Standing in the bathroom with its floral-patterned toilet, one remembers what Anne wrote about her adolescent preening. Even the chestnut tree which Anne looked at from her attic window has taken on significance. A fungus developed, causing its trunk to rot, so in 2006 the local council announced plans to chop it down. People from all over the world were outraged and in 2007 the 'Support Anne Frank Tree' foundation won a legal battle to preserve the tree, and its trunk was protected by an iron corset. Unfortunately, this was not the end of the story. On Monday 22 August 2010 the tree was destroyed during a heavy storm. Branches, cuttings and photographs of it quickly appeared for sale.[50]

Across Holland countless streets, schools, youth centres and other buildings bear the name Anne Frank. The Anne Frank Foundation, which was formed with the help of Otto Frank on 3 May 1957, the eve of Dutch National Memorial Day, maintains two travelling exhibits – 'Anne Frank in the World: 1929–1945' and 'Anne Frank: A History for Today' – which are viewed by thousands wherever they appear. They include photographs, a French grammar book and a pendant that belonged to Anne as a baby. The aims of the exhibitions are twofold: to educate audiences about the development of anti-Semitism in Nazi-occupied Europe and to warn people about the dangers of racism and prejudice. The foundation is also zealous in stopping the hijacking of Anne Frank's name for consumer enterprises, such as the attempt by a Spanish company to manufacture 'Anne Frank jeans'.[51]

In Britain, in 1998, trees were planted outside the British Library and Great Ormond Street Hospital for Children in London, to memorialise not only Anne Frank, but the countless other children killed during wars and persecution. More than 500 other trees have followed in towns, schools, libraries and other public places across Britain. In the courtyard of the British Library there is a bronze statue of Anne. The British branch of the Anne Frank Trust continues to battle racism and prejudice; it conducts outreach work in schools and other institutions, including prisons.

The experiences of a frightened child in hiding for her life have also inspired figures such as Nelson Mandela who, in a public address as president of the newly democratic South Africa in 1994, stated that he derived strength from her memory whilst he was imprisoned on Robben Island. *Time* magazine hailed her as one of the twenty 'heroes and icons of the 20th century', along with such figures as Albert Einstein. To mark the seventieth anniversary of her death, a new theatre production of her diary was staged in Amsterdam – it opened to standing ovations. Anne Frank has in many ways become a modern-day saint and her star shows no sign of waning. Children from all around the world continue to write letters to Anne Frank as if she is their friend – she remains irrevocably the eternal child.

One important aspect of the diary is that it stops before deportation and therefore allows us not to read about what happened to Anne and her family outside the 'safety' of the Secret Annexe. The critic Cynthia Ozick has famously written: 'Because the end is missing, the story of Anne Frank has been infantilised, Americanised, homogenised, sentimentalised, falsified, kitschified, and in fact, blatantly – arrogantly denied.'[52] Not only does the prevalence of Anne's widely circulated photograph make her seem almost familiar, but the 'personal' connotations of diary writing allow many of us to feel that Anne might be someone we could have known and been friends with. But in truth we still know very little about what she really thought and felt. She herself was aware of the impossibility of conveying the enormity of the events she was forced to live through:

I could spend hours telling you about the suffering the war has brought, but I'd only make myself more miserable. All we can do is wait, as calmly as possible, for it to end. Jews and Christians alike are waiting, the whole world is waiting, and many are waiting for death. (Wednesday 13 January 1943)

In addition to Anne's own diary we have Otto Frank's and Miep Gies's memories of Anne, as well as many of those of her school friends. Photographs from Otto's scrapbook show Anne developing from babyhood to early adolescence. They remind us of Anne's life before the war. Diaries of other children in hiding and academic research on the experiences of Jews in hiding give us an insight into the traumas of living in fear. Whilst we do not know what Anne herself felt during her imprisonment in Westerbork, Auschwitz or her last weeks in Bergen–Belsen, the accounts of the women who knew her in those places – of Hannah Pick-Goslar and Janny Brandes-Brilleslijper – and the writings of other prisoners as well as the reflections of the liberators help us in some way to imagine the unimaginable.

One of the attractions of the diary is that it allows us supposedly to read about the Holocaust whilst not actually having to deal with its horrors. It shows a bright, vivacious young girl who, although suffering the misery and stress of hiding in cramped and difficult conditions, still managed to write about more mundane concerns, such as adolescent infatuations and parental disagreements. Reading her diary, we are almost tempted to suspend what we actually know about her short life and hope she somehow manages to escape the death that so many were waiting for. Indeed, Harry James Cargas, an American academic and theologian who writes and teaches on the Holocaust, has confessed: 'Each time I read the *Diary* I cannot help but feel that this time she'll make it, she'll survive.'[53] Yet, if we are to honour the memory of those who died during the Holocaust, it is important to remember that she did not. Like 6 million other men, women and children, she was murdered for no other reason than that she was Jewish.

The desire for a different outcome is so intense that a number of books have been published suggesting that Anne Frank and her family *could* have survived. One is entitled *The Frank Family that Survived*. It tells of another family's experience of hiding in the Netherlands and claims to follow 'the same route Anne Frank might have taken had she not been betrayed'.[54] In a similar vein is *Eva's Story: A Survivor's Tale by the Stepsister of Anne Frank*, written by Eva Schloss. The title is in many ways misleading as Eva only became Anne's stepsister posthumously when Otto married Elfriede Markovits in 1953. What these experiences do have in common, however, is that they are set far apart from the genocide in Eastern Europe where the vast majority of the victims lived and where conditions were far harsher. Anne was able to realise this: 'When I think about our lives here, I usually come to the conclusion that we live in a paradise compared with the Jews who aren't in hiding' (Sunday 2 May 1943).

The afterlife of Anne Frank has also become a fruitful subject for literature. Philip Roth's *The Ghost Writer* imagines the consequences of Anne's survival, and Ellen Feldman's *The Boy Who Loved Anne Frank: A Novel* explores the life Peter van Pels might have lived under an assumed name as a non-Jewish refugee in America. The unbearable historical fact of lives cruelly cut short has become something of a literary obsession. Indeed, Nathan Englander's *What We Talk About When We Talk About Anne Frank* offers a satirical treatment of America's obsession, not just with Anne Frank, but with the Holocaust itself. Two Jewish couples play what they call the 'Anne Frank game' in which they speculate on which of their neighbours they could turn to to hide them in the event of another Holocaust. Englander perhaps epitomises a generational shift where writers and other artists are beginning to experiment with more irreverent treatments of Anne Frank and the Holocaust.

We are nearing a time when there will no longer be any witnesses to the Holocaust still alive. Miep Gies, who did all she could to save the Frank family, died in 2010 at the age of 100. This means that it is now left to us – those born after the events – to confront the daunting task of retrieving some sort of meaning from what happened. Through no fault of her own, the life of Anne Frank has been dehistoricised to such an extent that she has become a symbol, not just of the Holocaust, but of more recent examples of ethnic cleansing and genocide. For example, when a young girl named Zlata Fílípović wrote her diary (1991–93) detailing the siege of Sarajevo which took place during the war in the Balkans she was dubbed the 'Anne Frank of Sarajevo'.[55] Fílípović credits Frank as inspiring her to write a diary as she chronicles the unfolding violence and destruction of Sarajevo, but also realises the irony of her accolade, hoping 'that I will not suffer the fate of Anne Frank'.[56] She was in fact able to do what Anne Frank could only dream of: she escaped to Paris with her family. Fílípović is one of a myriad of other Anne Franks around the world, from Hadiya the 'Anne Frank of Iraq' to Hélène Beer the 'Anne Frank of France'.

If comparisons with Anne Frank continue in this manner they will become so ubiquitous as to be meaningless. As such, it becomes more important than ever to treat the experiences of the victims of each and every episode of ethnic cleansing, genocide and war with the respect and cautious humility they deserve. Rather than treating Anne Frank as 'a symbol of the 6 million', each individual testimony reminds us, not only of the extremity and magnitude of the Holocaust, but also of the diverse and intensely personal nature of Holocaust experiences.

The stories of Anne Frank and the other inhabitants of the Secret Annexe provide a mere glimpse into the abyss. It is right to cherish the writings that somehow managed to survive the war, but we must also bear in mind the countless documents which have been lost forever. Among them is the diary of Anne's sister Margot, which we know existed but which has never been found. The vast majority of the victims of the Holocaust perished without ever putting pen to paper. Each of these was a living, breathing, individual.

Above all, we must resist the urge to replace grim reality with fantasy. To hang on to Anne's oft-quoted line that 'people are really good at heart' and to focus too heavily on the brave men and women who sheltered her family is to overlook those who betrayed her and those who murdered her, and with that the final, terrible chapter in her life. The person who wrote those words met the same fate as thousands of other prisoners. Her diary stops before the last appalling months of her life unfold – our interest in the Holocaust must not.

But how should we preserve the memory of Anne's life? Her diary contains emotions that many of us, young and old, can relate to. If we do not proclaim the fact that a young girl managed to put pen to paper in such terrible times as an example of 'the triumph of the human spirit', should we instead focus solely on the tragedy of her untimely and brutal death? This question, of course, does not just apply to her diary; it relates to the numerous other documents bearing witness to these terrible times. As well as the diaries and other writings produced during the war – in the ghettos and the concentration camps as well as the places of secret hiding – we are fortunate to have the testimonies of the men and women who, against all odds, survived the war. As such, Anne Frank's story is one among thousands we now possess.

To reduce these lives to either a tale of human spirit or an unspeakable tragedy is to disregard their complex humanity, their individuality, the fact that they were more than their deaths.

What these beleaguered witnesses have in common is the commitment not only to document the suffering they were enduring and the atrocities they were forced to experience, but that despite everything they wished to retrieve some meaning from what they were made to endure. Anne Frank's diary – like the other testimonies

– should be read for its own sake: not because Anne is a symbol of the Holocaust but because its writer was a gifted author who lived through and reflected on a terrible chapter in human history.

Notes

1   Frank, O. H. and Pressler, M. (eds), *The Diary of a Young Girl: The Definitive Edition*, (London, 1997)

2   *Daily Telegraph*, 6 June 2009.

3   'Secret Annexe' is not the exact translation. *Het Achterhuis* literally means 'the house behind'.

4   Cited in Kirshenblatt-Gimblett, B. & Shandler, J. (eds), *Anne Frank Unbound: Media, Imagination, Memory* (Indiana University Press, 2002), p. 2.

5   The Frank family commissioned a professional photographer to make an annual photographic record of their daughters growing up.

6   Frank, A., *Anne Frank: The Diary of a Young Girl*, trans. B.M. Mooyaart-Doubleday (Doubleday, 1952).

7   This edition does not, however, include the pseudonyms Anne invented for herself nor indicate where she herself made alterations to the text. Anne's spelling and grammatical errors are also corrected.

8   Müller, M., *Anne Frank: The Biography*, trans. Kimber, R. and Kimer, R. (Bloomsbury, 1999).

9   Reisz, M., 'The Odour of Sanctity: A New Look at Anne Frank's Diary', *Jewish Quarterly* (Summer 1997), pp. 41–3.

10 Promotional films on how to use the products to make jam are now on show at the Anne Frank Museum.

11 Gies, M., with A.L. Gold, *Anne Frank Remembered: The Story of the Woman Who Helped to Hide the Frank Family* (Simon & Schuster, 1988), p. 79.

12 The Montessori school Anne attended is now named the Anne Frank School.

13 Lee, C.A., *Anne Frank and the Children of the Holocaust* (Puffin, 2006), p. 85.

14 Roseman, M., *The Villa, the Lake, the Meeting: Wannsee and the Final Solution* (Penguin, 2002).

15 Lee, *Anne Frank and the Children of the Holocaust*, p. 106.

16 Lee, C.A., *Roses from the Earth: The Biography of Anne Frank* (Penguin, 1999), p. 75.

17 Wolf, D.L., *Beyond Anne Frank: Hidden Children and Postwar Families in Holland* (University of California Press, 2007), p. 140.

18 In Holland, organisations such as the Amsterdamse Studentengroup and the Naamloze Vennootschap (NV) were formed solely to save Jewish children.

19 Bettleheim, B., 'The Ignored Lesson of Anne Frank', in H.A. Enzer & S. Solotaroff-Enzer, *Anne Frank: Reflections on her Life and Legacy* (University of Illinois Press, 2000), pp. 186–7.

20 Gies and Gold, *Anne Frank Remembered*, p. 70.

21 Bep Voskuijl, interview, *Rosita* (1960).

22 Lee, *Roses from the Earth*, p. 129.

23 Shapiro, E., 'The Reminiscences of Victor Kugler, the "Mr Kraler" of Anne Frank's Diary', *Yad Vashem Studies*, vol. 13 (1979), p. 360.

24 Presser, J., *The Destruction of the Dutch Jews* (E.P. Dutton, 1969).

25 Schnabel, E., 'Visiting Hours after 9 A.M.', in Enzer & Solotaroff-Enzer, *Anne Frank*, p. 46.

26 Lee, C.A., *The Hidden Life of Otto Frank* (Penguin, 2003), p. 75.

27 Lindwer, W., *The Last Seven Months of Anne Frank*, trans. Alison Meersshaert (Pantheon, 1991), p. 55.

28 Frank, *Memoir*.

29 Ibid.

30 Lindwer, *The Last Seven Months of Anne Frank*, p. 192.

31 Shephard, B., *After Daybreak: The Liberation of Belsen, 1945* (Jonathan Cape, 2005), p. 42.

32 Lee, *Roses from the Earth*, p. 198.

33 Michalczyk, J.J., *Filming the End of the Holocaust: Allied Documentaries, Nuremberg and the Liberation of the Concentration Camps* (Bloomsbury, 2014), p. 32.

34 Ibid.

35 Lindwer, *The Last Seven Months of Anne Frank*, p. 27.

36 Ibid., pp. 103–4.

37 Ibid., p. 74.

38 Ibid., pp. 27–8.

39 See Lustiger Thaler, H. & Wiedmann, W., 'Hauntings of Anne Frank: Sitings in Germany', in Kirshenblatt-

Gimblett and Shandler (eds), *Anne Frank Unbound: Media, Imagination, Memory* (Indiana University Press, 2002), pp. 137–57.

40 After Anne had filled the original notebook given to her on her birthday, she used an exercise book given to her by Miep Gies and also one of Margot's chemistry exercise books.

41 Gies & Gold, *Anne Frank Remembered*, p. 246.

42 Wolf, *Beyond Anne Frank*, p. 126.

43 Lee, *Roses from the Earth*, pp. 210–1.

44 Ibid., p. 214.

45 The article, published on 3 April 1946, in *Het Parool*, is reprinted in full in Barnouw, D., Paape, H. & van der Stroom, G. (eds), *The Diary of Anne Frank: The Critical Edition* (Netherlands State Institute for War Documentation, 1986), pp. 67–8.

46 Lee, *Roses from the Earth*, p. 226.

47 Faurisson, R., 'Is the Diary of Anne Frank Genuine?' *Journal for Historical Review*, vol. 3, no. 2 (Spring 1982). Cited in Sion, B., 'Anne Frank as Icon', in Kirshenblatt-Gimblett and Shandler (eds), *Anne Frank Unbound*, p. 188.

48 Ibid., 188–9.

49 Wiesenthal, S., 'Epilogue to the Diary of Anne Frank', in Enzer & Soltaroff-Enzer, *Anne Frank Unbound: Media, Imagination, Memory* (Indiana University Press, 2002), p. 68.

50 On this subject, see Kirshenblatt-Gimblett, B., 'Epilogue: A Life of Its Own – The Anne Frank Tree', in

Kirshenblatt-Gimblett & Shandler (eds), *Anne Frank Unbound: Media, Imagination, Memory* (Indiana University Press, 2002), pp. 324–38.

51 Lee, *Roses from the Earth*, pp. 233–4.

52 Ozick, C., 'Who Owns Anne Frank?' *New Yorker*, 6 October 1997, p. 87.

53 Rosenfeld, A., *The Americanisation of the Holocaust* (University of Michigan, 1995), p. 126.

54 Sander, G.F., *The Frank Family that Survived* (Cornell University Press, 2008). Other books in this vein include: Goslar, H. & Gold, A.L., *Hanneli Goslar Remembers: A Childhood Friend of Anne Frank* (Bloomsbury, 1999); van Maarsen, J., *Inheriting Anne Frank* (Arcadia Books, 2009); and Still, J., *And Then They Came for Me: Remembering the World of Anne Frank* (Dramatic Publishing, 1999).

55 Fílípović, Z., *Zlata's Diary: A Child's Life in Sarajevo*, trans. C. Pribichevich-Zorić (Viking, 1994).

56 Horowitz, S.R., 'Literary Afterlives of Anne Frank', in Kirshenblatt-Gimblett & Shandler (eds), *Anne Frank Unbound: Media, Imagination, Memory* (Indiana University Press), p. 244.

Timeline

1929	12 June: Anneliese Marie Frank born in Frankfurt-am-Main, Germany, the second daughter of Otto Frank and Edith Holländer
1933	30 January: Adolf Hitler is appointed Chancellor of Germany
	December: The Frank family leave Germany and settle in Amsterdam
1935	Nuremberg race laws prohibiting marriage and sexual relations between German Jews and 'Aryans'
1938	9 November: Kristallnacht (the Night of Broken Glass). A wave of anti-Jewish violence throughout Germany, Austria and areas of the Sudetenland in Czechoslovakia occupied by German troops
1939	1 September: Germany invades Poland. Three days later England and France declare war on Germany
1940	10 May: Germany invades Holland, Belgium and France. Four days later, Holland surrenders
1942	20 January: Wannsee Conference to co-ordinate the 'Final Solution'

	6 July: The Frank family go into hiding
	14 July: Dutch Jews start being deported to Auschwitz–Birkenau
1944	6 June: D-Day. Allied forces land in Normandy
	4 August: The inhabitants of the Secret Annexe are arrested and taken to Westerbork
	3 September: The Franks are put on the last train to Auschwitz
	October: Anne and Margot are transferred from Auschwitz–Birkenau to Bergen–Belsen
1945	6 January: Edith dies in Auschwitz
	Margot and Anne die in Bergen–Belsen sometime between February and March, just weeks before the camp is liberated by the British
1947	*Het Achterhuis* is published
1955	The play *The Diary of Anne Frank* by Frances Goodrich and Albert Hackett opens in New York
1959	The Hollywood film of *The Diary of Anne Frank*, produced and directed by George Stevens, appears throughout the United States
1960	The Anne Frank House officially opens to the public
1980	19 August: Otto Frank dies
1986	*The Diary of Anne Frank: The Critical Edition* is published in Dutch by the Netherlands State Institute for War Documentation. It is translated into English in 1989

1995   March: for the fiftieth anniversary of Anne
Frank's death, *The Diary of a Young Girl: The
Definitive Edition* is published in English

Further Reading

Bardgett, Suzanne & Cesarani, David (eds), *Belsen 1945: New Historical Perspectives* (Vallentine Mitchell, 2006)

Barnouw, David, Paape, Harry & van der Stroom, Gerrold, *The Diary of Anne Frank: The Critical Edition* (Netherlands State Institute for War Documentation, 1986)

Boonstra, Janrese & Rijnders, Marie-Jose (eds), *Anne Frank House: A Museum with a Story*, trans. Nancy Forest-Flier (Anne Frank Sitchting, 1992)

Frank, Anne, *Anne Frank: The Diary of a Young Girl*, trans. B.M. Mooyaart-Doubleday (Doubleday, 1952)

Frank, Anne, *Tales from the Secret Annexe* (Penguin, 1988)

Gies, Miep, with Alison Leslie Gold, *Anne Frank Remembered: The Story of the Woman Who Helped to Hide the Frank Family* (Simon and Schuster, 1988)

Goslar, Hanneli & Gold, Alison Leslie, *Hanneli Goslar Remembers: A Childhood Friend of Anne Frank* (Bloomsbury, 1999)

Graver, Lawrence, *An Obsession with Anne Frank: Meyer Levin and the Diary* (University of California Press, 1995)

Joods Historisch Museum, *Documents of the Persecution of the Dutch Jewry 1940–1945* (Joods Historisch Museum, 1979)

Kirshenblatt-Gimblett, Barbara & Shandler, Jeffrey (eds), *Anne Frank Unbound: Media, Imagination, Memory* (Indiana University Press, 2012)

Lee, Carol Ann, *Roses from the Earth: The Biography of Anne Frank 1929–1945* (Penguin, 1999)

Lee, Carol Ann, *The Hidden Life of Otto Frank* (Penguin, 2003)

Lindwer, Willy, *The Last Seven Months of Anne Frank*, trans. Alison Meersshaert (Pantheon, 1991)

Müller, Melissa, *Anne Frank: The Bibliography*, trans. Rita Kimber & Robert Kimber (Bloomsbury, 1999)

Roseman, Mark, *The Villa, the Lake, the Meeting: Wannsee and the Final Solution* (Penguin, 2002)

Waxman, Zoë, *Writing the Holocaust: Memory, Testimony, Representation* (Oxford University Press, 2008)

Wolf, Diane L., *Beyond Anne Frank: Hidden Children and Postwar Families in Holland* (University of California Press, 2007)

Web Links

About Anne Frank and her Life

www.annefrank.org – Website of the Anne Frank Museum in Amsterdam

www.annefrank.org.uk – Website of the Anne Frank Trust UK

www.annefrankguide.net – A guide for Anne Frank and the Second World War

www.annefrank.org/en/News/Anne-Frank-Tree/ – The Anne Frank Tree foundation

About the Holocaust

www.het.org.uk – Website of the Holocaust Educational Trust

www.hiddenlikeannefrank.com – Stories of other Jewish children in the Netherlands who went into hiding

www.holocaust-history.org – The Holocaust History

Project, an archive of documents, photographs, recordings, videos and essays about the Holocaust

www.iwm.org.uk/exhibitions/iwm-london/the-holocaust-exhibition – Website of the permanent Holocaust Exhibition at the Imperial War Museum in London

www.nizkor.org – The Nizkor Project, dedicated to the Holocaust victims

http://remember.org – A people's history of the Holocaust and genocide

www.ushmm.org – Website of the United States Holocaust Memorial Museum

www.yadvashem.org – Website of Yad Vashem, the Jewish people's living memorial to the Holocaust